Wedding Ring, Pickle Dish & More

Paper Piecing Curves

By Carolyn Cullinan McCormick

Wedding Ring, Pickle Dish & More
PAPER PIECING CURVES

Author: Carolyn Cullinan McCormick
Editor: Edie McGinnis
Technical Editor: Jane Miller
Designer: Amy Robertson
Photographer: Aaron T. Leimkuehler
Illustrator: Lon Eric Craven
Production Assistant: Jo Ann Groves

Published by:
Kansas City Star Books
1729 Grand Blvd.
Kansas City, Missouri, USA 64108

First edition, first printing
ISBN Number: 9781935362029
Library of Congress Control Number: 2008942685
Printed in the United States of America by
Walsworth Publishing Co., Marceline, MO

To order copies, call StarInfo at (816) 234-4636
and say "Books."

KANSAS CITY STAR
QUILTS
Continuing the Tradition

PickleDish.com
The Quilter's Home Page
www.PickleDish.com

*This book
is dedicated to Larry.
Every woman should be as lucky as I am
to have such a wonderful, supportive and
understanding husband. I am truly blessed!
I love you, Carolyn*

About the Author

Carolyn started to quilt in 1985 when she and her husband moved to Bozeman, Montana. There she worked and taught a variety of quilting and craft classes at The Patchworks from 1987 to 1995. In 1995, she invented the Add-A-Quarter ruler to make rotary cutting templates easier. The Add-A-Quarter has now become a standard tool when paper piecing.

Carolyn currently lives in Franktown, Colorado, outside of Denver with her husband, Larry. They have two children; Jennifer is busy planning her wedding to Anthony Marion, and Ryan and his wife, Megan, made the McCormicks first-time grandparents with the birth of their daughter, McKenna Carolyn.

This is the fourth book Carolyn has published with *The Kansas City Star.* Look for her other books: *Paper Piecing the Garden, Hard Times, Splendid Quilts* and *Quilts for Rosie.*

Contents

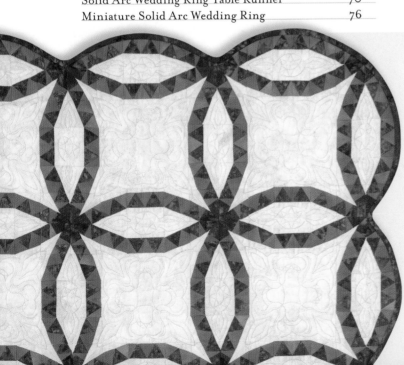

Acknowledgments

I am so very blessed to have a wonderful family. A special thanks to my daughter, Jennifer for all her help and my daughter-in-law, Megan for making the Wedding Ring and The Broken Stone quilts. Carol Netwal made the wonderful Pickle Dish. Marie Huber, my sister from Glendive, Montana, took the time to test "Jake."

Thanks to Megan McCormick, Parker, Colorado, Carol Netwal, Castle Rock, Colorado, Sandy Reinke, Lakewood, Colorado, Meriellen Joga, Castle Rock, Colorado, Kelly Collins, Littleton, Colorado and Connie Samora, Castle Rock, Colorado for taking a Saturday to help make the Wedding Ring quilt.

I am lucky to have special friends that made quilts for this book. Thank you everyone for taking the time to test the quilt directions: Julie Lilly, Monument, Colorado, Marilyn Vap, Castle Rock, Colorado, Kelly Collins, Littleton, Colorado, Pat Prestridge, San Antonio, Texas, Meriellen Joga, Castle Rock, Colorado, Brenda Phillips, Sedalia, Colorado, Polly Somers, Sedalia, Colorado and Jeannine Glendenning, Castle Rock, Colorado, Kathy Rutkosky, Larkspur, Colorado, Carol Bonetti, Castle Rock, Colorado, and Karon Larson, LaCrosse, Wisconsin.

Thanks to the following ladies for long arm quilting; Jan Korytkowski, Castle Rock, Colorado, Susan Bateman, Parker, Colorado and Jan Holden, Glendive, Montana. A special thanks to Carol Willey. Not only did she do a fabulous job but quilted many of the quilts under a very tight deadline.

I would like to thank the following people and the companies that they represent for their generous donations of fabrics, batting and thread. Leah Nelson from In The Beginning Fabrics, Emily Cohen from Timeless Treasures, LeeAnne Metz from Batik Textiles, Pati Violick from Marcus Brothers, Dawn Pereira from The Warm Company and Karlyn Allen with Presencia Thread.

Thanks to the staff at *The Kansas City Star*; Doug Weaver for giving me the opportunity to work with *The Kansas City Star* patterns. Edie McGinnis, my editor, who never fails to do a wonderful job. I appreciate her friendship as well as her advice and expertise. Working with Edie is always a joy!

Thanks to Eric Craven for his excellent technical illustrations. Thanks to Amy Robertson for her fabulous design work on this book and Aaron Leimkuehler, our photographer, for the great photos. I appreciate Jo Ann Groves for all the work she does on enhancing the photos. Many thanks go to Jane Miller for her wonderful technical editing skills.

— *Carolyn Cullinan McCormick*

"Miniature Solid Arc Wedding Ring" made and quilted by Carolyn Cullinan McCormick.

Introduction

A longtime dream and a new challenge come together in these patterns

It has always been a dream of mine to make a Wedding Ring quilt. I have tried making two of them in the past and both ended up in my "to-finish" box. It's a difficult quilt to make and I have seen many tops that have bubbles and bulges. The errors were too many and too large to ever hope that one could just "quilt them down."

Pickle Dish is another one of those quilts that fall into the same category. Difficult barely begins to describe this pattern. Little, tiny triangles are sewn together, then stitched on to curved pieces of background fabric. I'm in awe when I consider the quilts made using this pattern from the '30s and the women who made them. I can only imagine the amount of time it must have taken to cut out the triangles using a pair of scissors rather than having a rotary cutter at hand.

The Interlocked Wedding Rings is a quilt design that was shown for the month of April in the Montana Historical Society calendar for 2008. The quilt was designed by Elmer Williams of Great Falls, Montana, in the 1930s, and it was sewn together by his wife, Lizzie Williams. After seeing the traditional Wedding Ring quilt, Elmer felt that the rings should interlock, thus coming up with this unique design. The quilt is currently owned by Cecelia Goodman; Bozeman, Montana.

Not too long ago my editor asked if I thought I could design a paper pieced wedding ring quilt. Paper piecing curves — now there was a challenge if I ever heard one. I hemmed and hawed around a bit and said I would try. No promises.

The more I thought about it the more intriguing I found the idea. I had seen some patterns that had the rings paper pieced but you always had to sew them on to a curved center piece which left a lot of room for error. Hmmmmm, what if I could eliminate that problematic portion and actually make these curved patterns into paper pieced realities!

So the adventure began. After much trial and more than a few errors, I came up with workable patterns that actually make paper piecing curved patterns fun. And they are far easier to make than when one uses the old methods.

Not too long ago my editor asked if I thought I could design a paper pieced wedding ring quilt. Paper piecing curves — now there was a challenge if I ever heard one. I hemmed and hawed around a bit and said I would try. No promises.

The more I thought about it the more intriguing I found the idea. I had seen some patterns that had the rings paper pieced but you always had to sew them on to a curved center piece which left a lot of room for error. Hmmmmm, what if I could eliminate that problematic portion and actually make these curved patterns into paper pieced realities!

So the adventure began. After much trial and more than a few errors, I came up with workable patterns that actually make paper piecing curved patterns fun. And they are far easier to make than when one uses the old methods.

Once I found I could paper piece a wedding ring quilt, I decided there was no point in stopping there. I might just as well see if it would work on other curved patterns. Consequently you will find The Flower Ring, Hands all 'Round, Rob Peter and Pay Paul, Four Leaf Clover, Lafayette Orange Peel, Solid Wedding Rings and The Broken Stone.

You'll find two quilts included called The Broken Stone. One is a tribute to Jake, our beloved English Pointer who lost his battle with cancer last year. We miss him.

My desire is to have more paper pieced Wedding Ring quilts made than were made during the 1930s. I have two; the rest are up to you.

Happy Quilting!
—Carolyn

"Pickle Dish" made by Carolyn Cullinan McCormick, quilted by Carol Willey, Castle Rock, Colorado.

How to Paper Piece

WHY PAPER PIECE?

Paper piecing is great for beginners as well as experienced quilters. One can make a wonderful quilt on their very first try since complicated patterns are broken down into easily managed steps. Sewing the fabric to paper makes matching points relatively easy and the paper stabilizes the fabric, enabling one to use even the smallest of scraps.

HOW TO PAPER PIECE:

GET READY...

Use a copy machine to copy your pattern. Make all of your copies from the same original and use the same copy machine. All copy machines distort to some extent so check your pattern by holding the original and the copy together with a light source behind the two sheets of paper. Make as many copies as necessary. It's nice to have a few extras in case you make an error. Use the lightest weight paper you can find. The heavier the paper, the more difficult it is to remove.

Set up your sewing machine. Use a 90/14 size needle and set the stitch length to 18 - 20 stitches per inch. The larger needle perforates the paper making it easier to tear off. The smaller stitches keep the seams from ripping out when you remove the paper.

Place a piece of muslin or scrap fabric on your ironing board. When you press the pieces, the ink from the copies can transfer onto your ironing board cover.

Make sure you have a light source nearby. The light on your sewing machine is usually adequate.

Remember when paper piecing, your pattern will be reversed.

GET SET...

Here is a familiar pattern... see Fig. A. Instead of templates with seam allowances as many of us are used to seeing, we have lines and numbers. The lines indicate where to sew and the numbers indicate the sequence in which to sew. The only seam allowances that are shown are the ones that go around either a block or a unit.

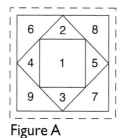

Figure A

The front of the pattern is where the lines and numbers are printed. This is the side you will sew on.

The back of the pattern is the side that is blank. This is where your fabric will be placed.

Cut your fabric pieces by following the cutting chart for each

PAPER PIECING SUPPLIES:
Add–A–Quarter Ruler — 10" Blocks
Add–An–Eighth Ruler — 4" Blocks
Rotary Cutter and Mat
Rulers for Rotary Cutting
Sewing Machine
90/14 Sewing Machine Needles
Thread
Iron and Ironing Board
Straight Pins (Regular, Silk
   and/or Flower Head)
Double–Sided tape (Optional)
Add-Enough or Piece of Template Plastic
   Measuring 3" x 10"
Tweezers
   (For removing small pieces
   of paper)
Paper for Foundation Piecing
   (This should be relatively thin)
Piece of Muslin or Scrap Fabric
   (For Ironing Board)

quilt. Always make sure the piece of fabric is at least 1/4" larger all the way around than shown on the foundation pattern.

SEW!

Put fabric number 1 **right side up** on the blank side of the pattern. You may either pin the piece in place or use double-sided tape to hold the fabric in place. The tape makes the fabric lie flat on the paper. The pin can make a small rise in the paper. **See Fig. B.**

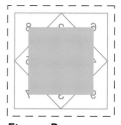

Figure B

Turn the foundation pattern over, look through the paper toward your light source and make sure the fabric extends over the lines on each side by at least 1/4". **See Fig. C.**

Place the Add-Enough or template plastic on the sewing line between piece number 1 and piece number 2. Fold back the foundation pattern over the edge of the plastic. You can now see the excess fabric from piece number 1. See Fig D.

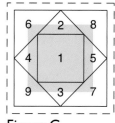

Figure C

Place the Add-A-Quarter ruler up against the fold of the foundation paper with lip side down. Use the rotary cutter to trim the extra fabric from piece number 1. You will now have a straight line to help you place fabric piece number 2. **See Fig. E.**

Now place the fabric that goes in position number 2 of the pattern on the trimmed edge of piece number 1 with the right sides facing each other. **See Fig. F.**

Turn the foundation paper over and stitch on the line between piece number 1 and piece number 2. Sew a few stitches before the line begins and a few stitches after the line ends. Make sure piece number 2 does not slip. **See Fig. G.**

Flip the paper back over and open piece number 2. Press the piece open using a dry iron. **See Fig. H.**

Fold the foundation paper back along the line between piece number 1 and piece number 3 using the Add-Enough or the template plastic. Butt the Add-A-Quarter up against the paper and trim the excess fabric. **See Fig. I.**

Turn the foundation back over and position fabric piece number 3, being careful not to displace your fabric. Sew on the line between number 1 and number 3. **See Fig. J & K.**

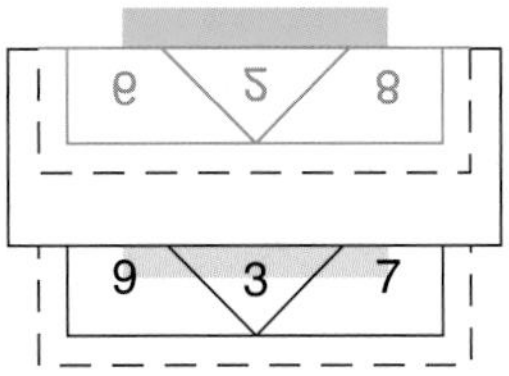

Continue sewing each piece in place in the numeric order given until all the pieces are sewn in place and each unit is complete. **See Fig. L.**

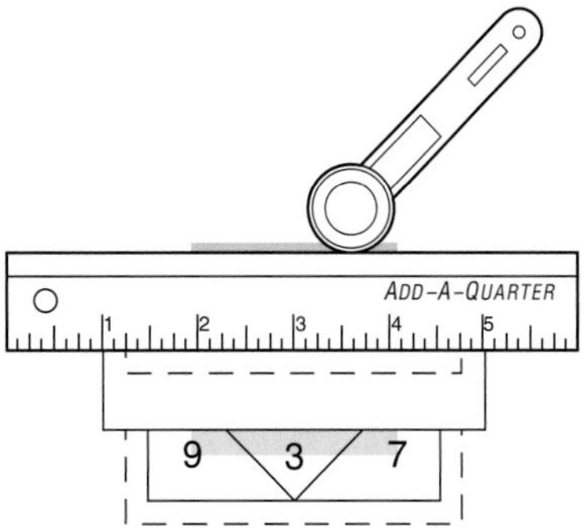

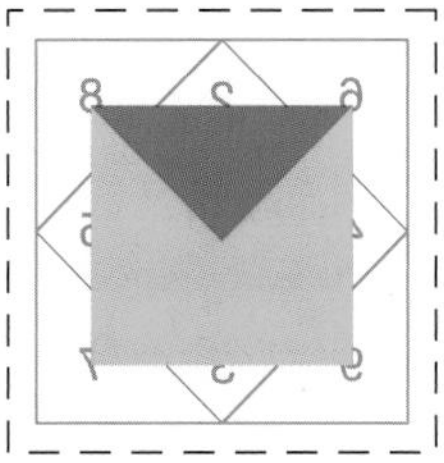

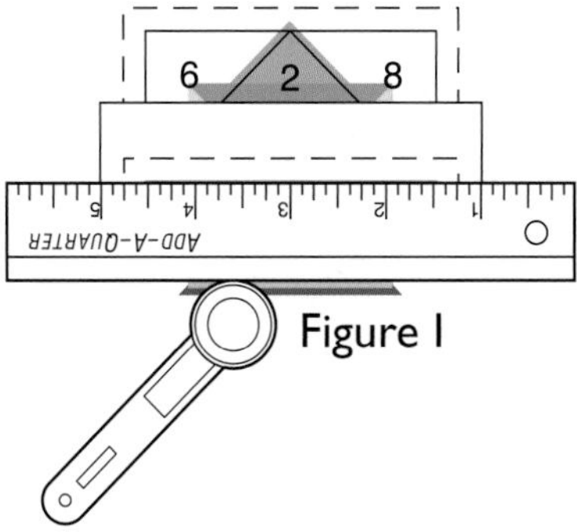

After all the pieces are sewn onto the foundation, you will be ready to trim the edges. You will need a 1/4" seam allowance around the entire block, no matter the size of the block, when you sew your blocks together. **Never trim on the solid line!** Line up the ruler with the solid line on the foundation. Trim off the excess fabric using your rotary cutter.

If you are paper piecing a block that is made up of multiple units, the time has come to sew them together. Pin the units together. Make sure the lines you are sewing match on the top and the bottom of the units. This can be accomplished by putting a pin straight through both lines at each intersection. Always check to make sure the seam is directly on the top line and the underneath line as well, otherwise your block will be off.

After you have sewn two units together and after pressing, remove the paper from the back side of the seam allowance, this will reduce some of the bulk.

When the block is finished, **do not remove the paper!** Since the fabrics are not always sewn on the straight of grain when paper piecing, it is best to join the blocks first. This gives you a sewing line to follow and stabilizes the blocks. Remove the paper after the blocks are sewn together. You might want to remove the really small pieces with a pair of tweezers.

Figure D

Figure E

Figure F

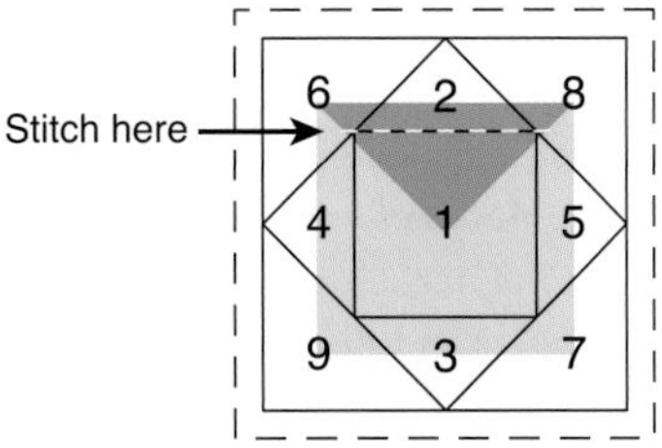

Stitch here →

Figure G

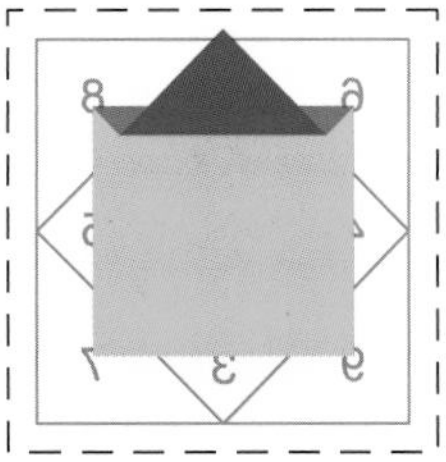

Figure H

Figure I

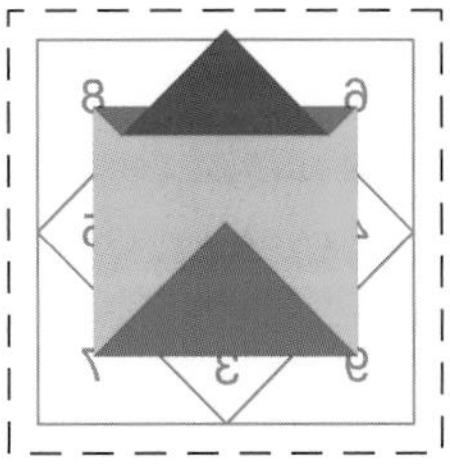

Figure J

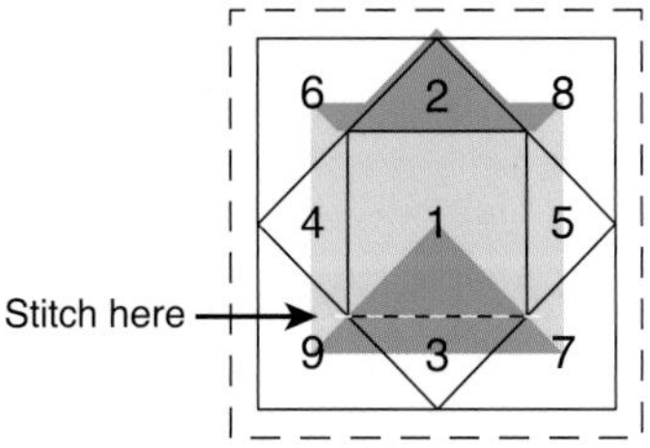

Stitch here →

Figure K

Figure L

How to Paper Piece

BORDERS

All the borders in this book are strips with straight cut seams. Cut the width of the fabric and follow the cutting chart for cutting requirements.

Measure the quilt from side to side in the center of the quilt. If the measurement is larger than the width of the fabric, piece the border strips together with a straight seam. Press. Cut two border strips to match the measurement. Pin on the border. Begin with pinning one end and then the other. Then pin in the middle and in both directions. This will allow for easing where necessary. If the paper is still on the fabric when sewing on the first border; sew with the paper facing up. This will give you a stitching line to follow and also will keep the border from stretching. Press.

Measure the quilt from top to bottom in the center of the quilt. Piece two strips together with a straight seam. Press. Cut two of the border strips to match the measurement. Pin and sew in place. Press.

If there is more than one border, follow the same procedure as above. If there is a problem with the fabrics stretching, try using a walking foot.

OPPOSING SEAMS

Always press the seams to one side. It will add strength to your quilt and distribute the bulk. Keep this rule in mind when sewing the units together. It will be easier to match the points and distribute the bulk.

PRESSING SUGGESTIONS

Pressing is an important part of paper piecing and, done correctly, will help ensure a more satisfactory quilt. Here are some suggestions to follow:

1. Use a hot dry iron when pressing the fabrics onto the units. Steam will make the paper curl. A steam iron works great when pressing the units that have been sewn together; the steam makes the paper more relaxed.
2. Place a piece of muslin on the ironing board to protect it from the ink that may come off of the paper when pressing.
3. Always press with the paper side down. Pressing on the paper will allow the ink to transfer to the iron and then onto your fabric, leaving black smudge.
4. The traditional way to press is always to the dark side. When paper piecing, this is not always the rule. When working with light fabric, you can avoid a line from the dark fabric showing through by extending the light fabric slightly over the dark.

VARIATIONS...

Since these patterns from *The Kansas City Star* have been adapted to a paper pieced pattern from traditional blocks, you will have a few things crop up that you might not run into with blocks that were originally designed with paper piecing in mind.

You may have triangles that are either sewn to inside or outside corners of the block. These are shown as separate pieces. You may either pin or use double-sided tape to hold your fabric to the triangles. Sew them in the order indicated on the pattern leaving the paper in place.

Use half-square triangles where you see this symbol:

SOME SUGGESTIONS...

If you have to unsew and the paper foundation separates on the sewing line, use a piece of clear tape to repair the pattern.

Sometimes you will notice the stitches from the previously sewn fabric when you fold back the foundation. If this happens, just pull the foundation away from the fabric and trim using the ruler.

To help speed up your paper piecing, place all of your position I pieces on multiple units at the same time. Trim and sew multiple units at the same time.

By placing your pattern face down on a white piece of paper you will be able to see the outline of the design for placement of your first fabric.

A FEW MORE THINGS

There are two options for the center pieces; they may be made using the paper template or to speed up the piecing cut the squares the correct size.

When figuring the number of strips required for each fabric, 40" was used as the standard width. Some fabrics may be wider and others may be shorter.

The strips are cut the width of the fabric. When cutting out the required pieces from each fabric, there may be pieces left over.

HOW TO FUSSY CUT SQUARES

Make a square template the desired size out of template plastic (do not add the seam allowances). Place the template over the pattern to be fussy cut, use permanent marker to outline the design. Place a couple pieces of rolled up masking tape to the back of the template. Working with only one layer of fabric, position the template on the design element you want to highlight in your quilt. Line up the template on the design, place the Add-A-Quarter™ ruler next to the template then cut each side of the square using your rotary cutter. Using the Add-A-Quarter will automatically add the 1/4" seam allowance.

BIAS BINDING

It is important to use bias binding for the quilts with curved outer edges; it has more stretch and will conform to the curve of the quilt.

MAKING BIAS BINDING

Start with 1/2 yard of fabric or a fat quarter. Press the fabric. Line up a ruler on the 45 degree line and make the first cut. Move the ruler to measure 2 1/2", cut. Continue until you have enough binding. A half yard will yield about 280" and a fat quarter will yield about 100".

Sew the strips together on the 45 degree angle. Press the binding in half, carefully matching the edges. Turn the end of the binding under 1/4" and press.

SEWING ON BIAS BINDING

Start with the end of the binding that has been pressed under 1/4". Leave about 4" of binding hanging loose. Begin sewing at the center of the outer curve. Stitch the binding around the curve. Ease in any fullness but do not stretch the binding.

Before getting to the inner point of two arcs, clip the seam allowance. Be very careful not to cut beyond the seam allowance. Line up the binding with the edge of the quilt; fold it back towards the top to expose the inner point of the arcs that have been clipped. Finger press then unfold the binding. With a pencil, mark the point that intersects with the finger pressing line and the clipped seam allowance. Sew the binding down to the mark, keep the needle down, pivot and continue stitching.

When you get back to the beginning of the binding, trim the end at a 45 degree angle. Leave the end long enough to be tucked into the piece that has been turned under 1/4". Continue sewing the remaining binding down.

After stitching the binding on by machine, fold the binding together at the inner points and stitch by hand 1/8" from the top of the fold. This will help the binding appear smooth at each inner point. Fold the binding to the back of the quilt and stitch in place by hand.

"Wedding Ring" made by Carolyn Cullinan McCormick,
quilted by Carol Willey, Castle Rock, Colorado.

Wedding Ring

October 1928 • 65" x 75" Quilted • 42 – 10" Blocks • 26 – Outside Curved Blocks

CUTTING INSTRUCTIONS

From the background fabric, cut:

* Paper

✳ 7 – 6" strips. Cut the strips into 42 – 6" squares.

** No Paper

✳ 6 – 5 1/2" strips. Cut the strips into 42 – 5 1/2" squares.

✳ 12 – 6" strips. Cut the strips into 194 – 2 1/4" x 6" rectangles.

✳ 7 – 3 1/4" strips. Cut the strips into 168 – 1 1/2" x 3 1/4" rectangles.

✳ 13 – 2 1/2" strips. Cut the strips into 336 – 1 1/2" x 2 1/2" rectangles.

✳ 15 – 2" strips. Cut 388 – 1 1/2" x 2" rectangles.

From each of the 28 print fabrics, cut:
(If utilizing scraps, cut the following amount of pieces.)

✳ 2 – 3" x 18" strips. Cut the strips into 388 – 2" x 3" rectangles.

✳ 1 – 2 3/4" x 18" strip. Cut the strip into 194 – 2 1/4" x 2 3/4" rectangles.

✳ 2 – 2 1/2" x 18" strips. Cut the strips into 388 – 2 1/4" x 2 1/2" rectangles. These pieces must match with units B & G. (See sewing units together.)

✳ 2 – 2 1/2" x 18" strips. Cut the strips into 388 – 1 1/2" x 2 1/2" rectangles. These pieces must match with units A & F. (See sewing units together.)

From the green fabric, cut:

✳ 4 – 3 1/4" strips. Cut the strips into 42 – 3 1/4" squares. Cut the squares into half-square triangles.

SUPPLY LIST

Units A & B – Make 168 Copies
Units C & D – Make 84 Copies
Unit E – Make 42 Copies (If Using Paper)
Units F & G – Make 26 Copies
Units H & I – Make 14 Copies
Units J & K – Make 12 Copies

FABRICS:

Background	5 3/4 yd.
Print	28 Fat Quarters or Various Scraps
Pink	1/2 yd.
Green	
Blocks	1/2 yd.
Binding	1 yd.
Total:	1 1/2 yd.
Backing: 4 3/4 yds.	
Batting: 2 yds. 90" wide	

✳ 1 – 2 3/4" strip. Cut the strip into 13 – 2 3/4" squares. Cut the squares into half-square triangles.

From the pink fabric, cut:

✳ 4 – 3 1/4" strips. Cut the strips into 42 – 3 1/4" squares. Cut the squares into half-square triangles.

✳ 1 – 2 3/4" strips. Cut the strips into 13 – 2 3/4" squares. Cut the squares into half-square triangles.

BINDING:

From the green fabric, cut:

✳ 328" of 2 1/2" wide bias binding.

---

* Paper – if using the paper template use this measurement.

** No Paper – if not placing the fabric on the paper template that is provided use this measurement.

PATTERN ON PAGES 92–94.

Wedding Ring

POSITION CHART: 42 — 10" BLOCKS

	Fabric	Position	Size
Unit A – Make 168	Print	1	2 1/4" x 2 3/4"
	***Print	2,3	2 1/4" x 2 1/2"
	Background	4,5	1 1/2" x 2 1/2"
Unit B – Make 168	Background	1	2 1/4" x 6"
	***Print	2,3	1 1/2" x 2 1/2"
Unit C – Make 84	Background	1	1 1/2" x 3 1/4"
	Print	2,3	2" x 3"
	Background	4,5	1 1/2" x 2"
	Green	6	3 1/4" x 3 1/4" ◣
Unit D – Make 84	Background	1	1 1/2" x 3 1/4"
	Print	2,3	2" x 3"
	Background	4,5	1 1/2" x 2"
	Pink	6	3 1/4" x 3 1/4" ◣
Unit E – Make 42			
** No Paper	Background	1	5 1/2" x 5 1/2"
* Paper			6" x 6"

*** It is very important to remember when sewing the fabrics onto units B2 and B3 that they must correspond with the fabrics on units A2 and A3.

SEWING DIRECTIONS: 10" BLOCKS

1. Following the position chart sew all fabric onto the units A, B, C and D. If using paper for the center pieces (unit E) assemble as well.

2. It is very important to remember when sewing the fabrics onto units B2 and B3 that they must correspond with the fabrics on units A2 and A3.

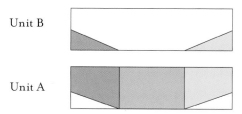

Unit B

Unit A

3. Trim the units leaving a ¼" seam allowance.

4. Sew units together following the diagram on how to assemble the block. Remove only the paper from the backside of the seam allowance; leave the remaining paper on until sewing the block to another block.

Sew units A to units B

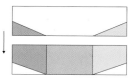

Make 21 - #1 blocks. **Note:** #1 and #2 blocks are all made using the same units. The only difference is the way they are pressed. Each block is pressed differently to make it easier for you to join the blocks together.

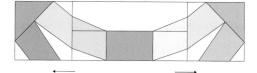

Sew units AB to each side of units E

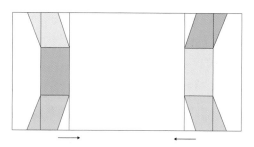

Sew together as shown

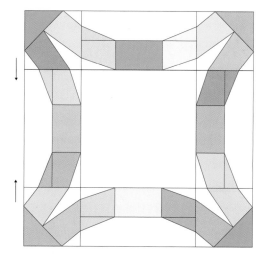

Make 21 – #2 blocks
Sew units C and D to each side of units AB
Make 42 following these pressing arrows.

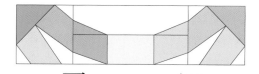

Sew units AB to each side of units E

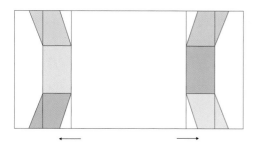

Sew together as shown

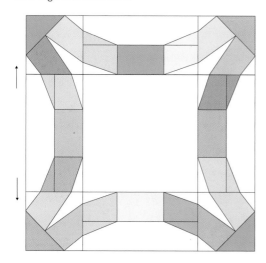

POSITION CHART: OUTSIDE CURVES, 26 CURVES

		Fabric	Position	Size
Unit F – Make 26		Print	1	2 1/4" x 2 3/4"
		***Print	2,3	2 1/4" x 2 1/2"
Unit G –Make 26		Background	1	2 1/4" x 6"
		***Print	2,3	1 1/2" x 2 1/2"
Unit H – Make 14		Print	1	2" x 3"
		Background	2	1 1/2" x 2"
		Pink	3	2 3/4" x 2 3/4"
Unit I – Make 14		Print	1	2" x 3"
		Background	2	1 1/2" x 2"
		Green	3	2 3/4" x 2 3/4"
Unit J –Make 12		Print	1	2" x 3"
		Background	2	1 1/2" x 2"
		Pink	3	2 3/4" x 2 ¾"
Unit K – Make 12		Print	1	2" x 3"
		Background	2	1 1/2" x 2"
		Green	3	2 3/4" x 2 3/4"

*** It is very important to remember when sewing the fabrics onto units G2 and G3 that they must correspond with the fabrics on units F2 and F3.

SEWING DIRECTIONS: OUTSIDE CURVED PIECES

1. Following the position chart sew all fabric onto the units F, G, H, I, J and K.

2. It is very important to remember when sewing the fabrics onto units G2 and G3 that they must correspond with the fabrics on units F2 and F3.

Unit G
Unit F

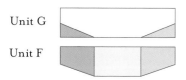

3. Trim the units leaving a ¼" seam allowance.

4. Sew units together following the diagram on how to assemble the curved block. Remove only the paper from the backside of the seam allowance; leave the remaining paper on until sewing the block to another block.

Make 26 - FGHI Outside Curves

Sew units F to units G

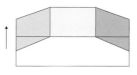

Sew units H and I to units FG
Make 7 - #3 blocks pressing as following.

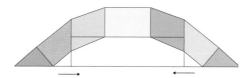

Wedding Ring

Make 7 - #4 blocks pressing as following.

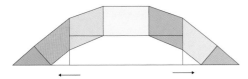

Sew units J and K to units FD
Make 6 - #5 blocks pressing as following.

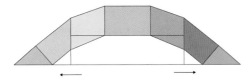

Make 6 - #6 blocks pressing as following.

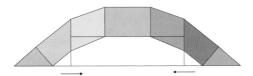

ASSEMBLING THE QUILT

1. Before assembling the quilt, it is very important to sew (stay stitch) 1/8" on the curve of the outside pieces. This will help stabilize the fabric when removing the paper.

2. Refer to the diagram and sew the outside curves to the blocks using a 1/4" seam allowance. Sew the blocks together in rows.

3. Gently remove the paper from the quilt, leaving the outside edges for last. When removing the paper, be very careful not to stretch the edges.

4. Quilt as desired.

5. Trim off the excess batting and backing.

6. Sew on the bias binding.

Wedding Ring

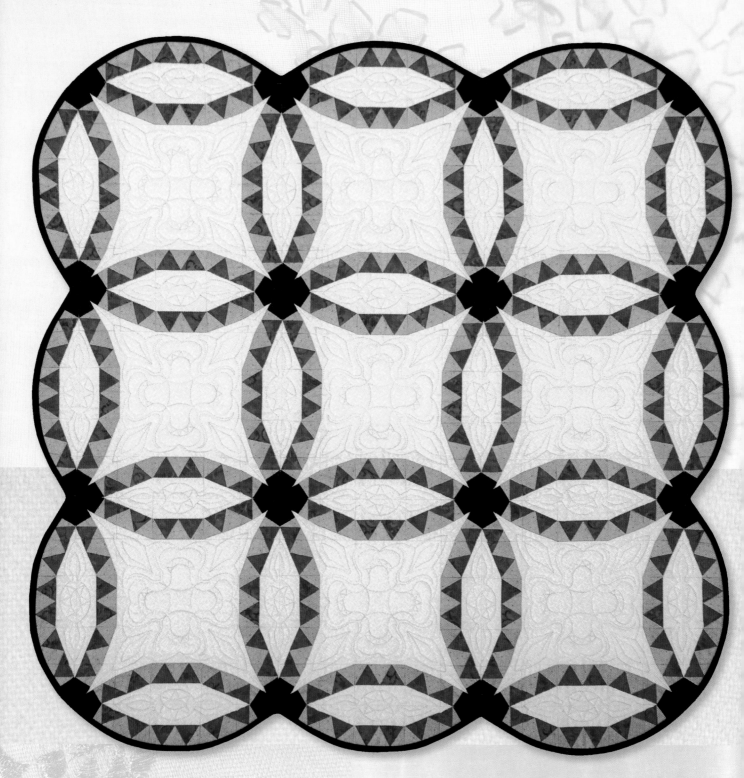

"Pickle Dish" made by Carolyn Cullinan McCormick, quilted by Carol Willey, Castle Rock, Colorado.

Pickle Dish

October 1931 • 33 1/2" x 33 1/2" Quilted • 9 – 10" Blocks • 12 – Outside Edge

CUTTING INSTRUCTIONS

From the background fabric, cut:

***Paper**

✽ 2 – 7" strips. Cut the strips into 9 – 7" squares.

****No Paper**

✽ 2 – 6 1/2" strips. Cut the strips into 9 – 6 1/2" squares.

✽ 3 – 3 1/2" strips. Cut the strips into 48 – 1 3/4" x 3 1/2" rectangles.

✽ 8 – 3" strips. Cut the strips into 96 – 1 3/4" x 3" rectangles and 72 – 1 1/2" x 3" rectangles.

✽ 3 – 2 3/4" strips. Cut the strips into 72 – 1 1/2" x 2 3/4" rectangles.

✽ 3 – 1 1/2" strips. Cut the strips into 96 – 1 1/4" x 1 1/2" rectangles.

From the taupe fabric, cut:

✽ 11 – 2 1/4" strips. Cut the strips into 48 – 2" x 2 1/4" rectangles, 96 – 1 3/4" x 2 1/4" rectangles and 96 – 1 1/2" x 2 1/4" rectangles.

✽ 9 – 2" strips. Cut the strips into 96 – 1 3/4" x 2" rectangles and 96 – 1 1/2" x 2" rectangles.

✽ 4 – 1 3/4" strips. Cut the strips into 96 – 1 1/2" x 1 3/4" rectangles.

From the red fabric, cut:

✽ 9 – 2" strips. Cut the strips into 96 – 2" squares and 96 – 1 1/2" x 2" rectangles.

✽ 5 – 2 1/4" strips. Cut the strips into 96 – 2" x 2 1/4" rectangles.

✽ 4 – 1 3/4" strips. Cut the strips into 96 – 1 1/2" x 1 3/4" rectangles.

From the black fabric, cut:

✽ 5 – 2 1/2" strips. Cut the strips into 96 – 1 3/4" x 2 1/2" rectangles

BINDING:

From the black fabric, cut:
148" – 2 1/2" bias binding.

PATTERN ON PAGES 95–97.

SUPPLY LIST

Units A, B, C, D & E – Make 36 Copies
Unit F – Make 9 Copies (If using Paper)
Unit G, H, I, J & K – Make 12 Copies

FABRICS:

Background	2 yds.
Taupe	1 5/8 yd.
Red	1 1/4 yd.
Black	
Blocks	1/2 yd.
Bias Binding	1/2 yd.
Total	1 yd.

Batting: 40" x 40"
Backing: 1 1/8 yds.

Pickle Dish

POSITION CHART: 9 – 10" BLOCKS

	Fabric	Position	Size
Unit A – Make 36	Taupe	1	2" x 2 1/4"
	Red	2,3	2" x 2"
	Taupe	4,5	1 1/2" x 2 1/4"
	Background	6	1 3/4" x 3 1/2"
Units B & C – Make 36 each	Red	1	2" x 2 1/4"
	Taupe	2	1 3/4" x 2 1/4"
	Taupe	3	1 3/4" x 2"
	Red	4	1 1/2" x 1 3/4"
	Background	5	1 1/2" x 2 3/4"
	Background	6	1 3/4" x 3"
Units D & E – Make 36 each	Black	1	1 3/4" x 2 1/2"
	Taupe	2	1 1/2" x 2"
	Red	3	1 1/2" x 2"
	Background	4	1 1/4" x 1 1/2"
	Taupe	5	1 1/2" x 1 3/4"
	Background	6	1 1/2" x 3"
Unit F – Make 9			
**No Paper	Background	1	6 1/2" x 6 1/2"
*Paper			7" x 7"

SEWING DIRECTIONS: 10" BLOCKS

1. Following the position chart sew all fabric onto units A, B, C, D and E. If using paper for the center pieces (unit F), assemble as well.

2. Trim the units leaving a 1/4" seam allowance.

3. Sew units together following the diagram on how to assemble the block. Remove only the paper from the backside of the seam allowance; leave the remaining paper on until sewing the block to another block.

   Make 9 Blocks – Blocks 1 and 2 are all made using the same units. The only difference is the way they are pressed. Each block is pressed differently to make it easier to join the blocks together.

   Sew units D to units E.

Block #1 – Make 5 following this pressing chart.

Sew units B and C to each side of units A. Press 20 following this pressing chart.

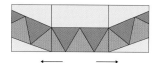

Sew units DE to each side of units ABC. Make 10 following this pressing chart.

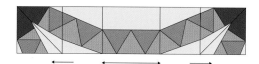

Sew units ABC to each side of units F. Make 5 following this pressing chart.

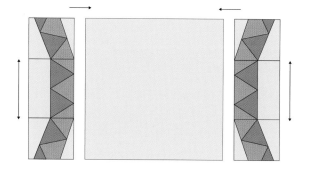

Add units ABCDE to the top and bottom.

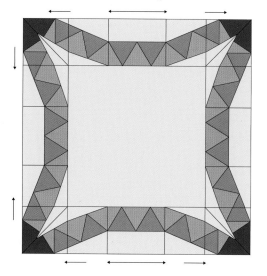

Block #2 – Make 4 following this pressing chart.

Sew units B and C to each side of units A.
Press 16 following this diagram.

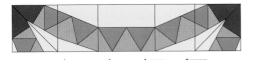

Sew units DE to each side of units ABC.
Make 8 following this pressing chart.

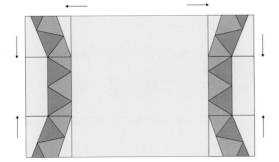

Sew units ABC to each side of unit F.
Make 4 following this pressing chart.

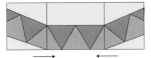

Add units ABCDE to the top and bottom.

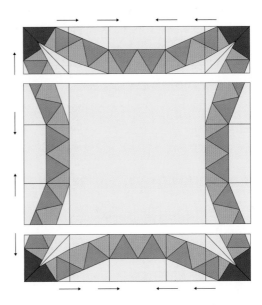

Pickle Dish

POSITION CHART: 12 – OUTSIDE CURVES	Fabric	Position	Size
Unit G – Make 12	Taupe	1	2" x 2 1/4"
	Red	2,3	2" x 2"
	Taupe	4,5	1 1/2" x 2 1/4"
	Background	6	1 3/4" x 3 1/2"
Units H & I – Make 12 each	Red	1	2" x 2 1/4"
	Taupe	2	1 3/4" x 2 1/4"
	Taupe	3	1 3/4" x 2"
	Red	4	1 1/2" x 1 3/4"
	Background	5	1 3/4" x 3"
Units J & K – Make 12 each	Black	1	1 3/4" x 2 1/2"
	Taupe	2	1 1/2" x 2"
	Red	3	1 1/2" x 2"
	Background	4	1 1/4" x 1 1/2"
	Taupe	5	1 1/2" x 1 3/4"

SEWING DIRECTIONS: 12 OUTSIDE CURVES

Sew units H and I to each side of units G.

Sew units J and units K to each side of units GHI.

Make 4 following this pressing chart.

Block #3

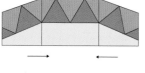

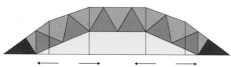

Make 4 following this pressing chart.

Block #4

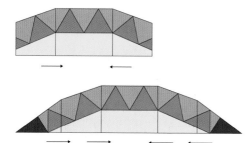

Make 2 following this pressing chart.

Block #5

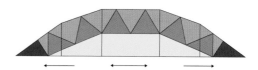

Make 2 following this pressing chart.

Block #6

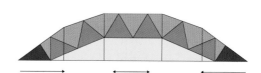

ASSEMBLING THE QUILT

1. Before assembling the quilt, it is very important sew (stay stitch) 1/8" on the curve of the outside pieces. This will help to stabilize the fabric when removing the paper.

2. Refer to the diagram and sew the outside curves to the blocks using a 1/4" seam allowance. Sew the blocks together in rows then sew the rows together.

3. Remove the paper from the quilt, leaving the paper on the outside edges until last. Be careful when removing the paper to avoid stretching the outside edges.

4. Quilt as desired.

5. Trim off excess batting and backing.

6. Sew on bias binding.

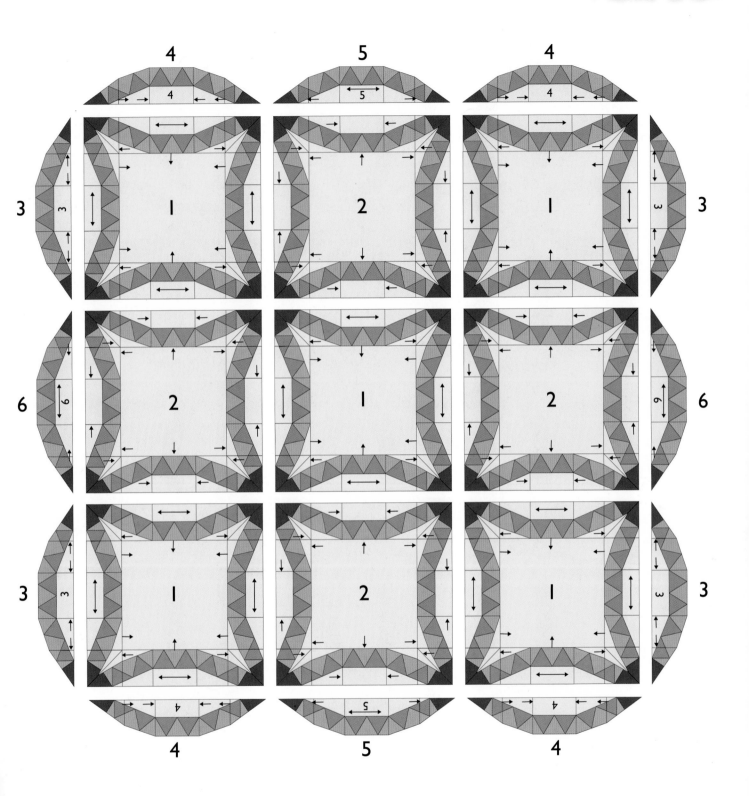

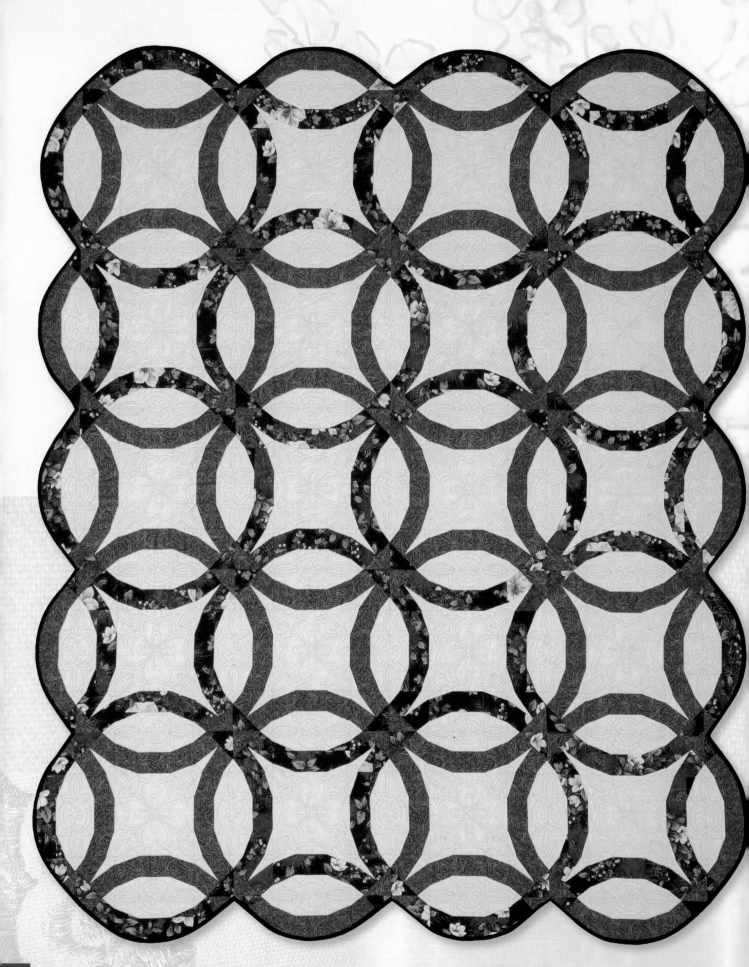

Solid Arc Wedding Ring

Variation of Wedding Ring October 1928 • 53" x 64 1/2" Quilted
20 – 12" Blocks • 9 – Medium Outside Edge • 9 – Dark Outside Edge

CUTTING INSTRUCTIONS

From the background fabric, cut:

✳ 7 – 7" strips. Cut the strips into 98 – 2 1/2" x 7" rectangles.

*Paper

✳ 4 – 7" strips. Cut the strips into 20 – 7" squares.

** No Paper

✳ 4 – 6 1/2" strips. Cut the strips into 20 – 6 1/2" squares.

✳ 4 – 3 3/4" strips. Cut the strips into 80 – 2" x 3 3/4" rectangles.

✳ 7 – 3" strips. Cut the strips into 160 – 1 1/2" x 3" rectangles.

✳ 8 – 2 1/4" strips. Cut the strips into 196 – 1 1/2" x 2 1/4" rectangles.

From the medium fabric, cut:

✳ 3 – 7" strips. Cut the strips into 49 – 2 1/4" x 7" rectangles.

✳ 7 – 3 1/2" strips. Cut the strips into 80 – 2 1/4" x 3 1/2" rectangles and 20 – 3 1/2" x 3 1/2" squares. Cut the squares into 40 half-square triangles.

✳ 2 – 3 1/4" strips. Cut the strips into 18 – 2 1/2" x 3 1/4" rectangles.

✳ 4 – 3" strips. Cut the strips 98 – 1 1/2" x 3"rectangles.

✳ 2 – 2 1/2" strips. Cut the strips into 18 – 2 1/4" x 2 1/2" rectangles.

From the dark fabric, cut:

✳ 3 – 7" strips. Cut the strips into 49 – 2 1/4" x 7" rectangles.

✳ 7 – 3 1/2" strips. Cut the strips into 80 – 2 1/4" x 3 1/2" rectangles and 20 – 3 1/2"squares. Cut the squares into 40 half-square triangles.

✳ 2 – 3 1/4" strips. Cut the strips into 18 – 2 1/2" x 3 1/4" rectangles.

✳ 4 – 3" strips. Cut the strips into 98 – 1 1/2" x 3" rectangles.

✳ 2 – 2 1/2" strips. Cut the strips into 18 – 2 1/4" x 2 1/2" rectangles.

SUPPLY LIST

Unit A – Make 80 Copies
Unit B – Make 80 Copies
Unit C – Make 20 Copies (If using Paper)
Unit D – Make 18 Copies
Unit E & F– Make 9 Copies Each
Unit G & H– Make 9 Copies Each

FABRICS:

Blocks

Background	3 7/8 yds.	
Medium	2 yds.	
Dark	2 yds.	

Binding

Black	1/2 yd.	

Batting: 1 3/4 yd. 90" wide
Backing: 4 1/8 yds.

BINDING:

From the black fabric, cut:
266" - 2 1/2" bias binding.

---

* Paper – if using the paper template use this measurement.

** No Paper – if not placing the fabric on the paper template that is provided use this measurement.

PATTERN ON PAGES 98–100.

Opposite: "Solid Arc Wedding Ring" made by Carolyn Cullinan McCormick, quilted by Carol Willey, Castle Rock, Colorado. Fabric by Timeless Treasures.

Solid Arc Wedding Ring

POSITION CHART: 20 -12" BLOCKS

	Fabric	Position	Size
Unit A – Make 40 Medium	Background	1	2 1/2" x 7"
	Medium	2,3	1 1/2" x 3"
	Medium	4	2 1/4" x 7"
	Background	5,6	1 1/2" x 3"
Unit A – Make 40 Dark	Background	1	2 1/2" x 7"
	Dark	2,3	1 1/2" x 3"
	Dark	4	2 1/4" x 7"
	Background	5,6	1 1/2" x 3"
Unit B – Make 40 Medium	Background	1	2" x 3 3/4"
	Medium	2,3	2 1/4" x 3 1/2"
	Background	4,5	1 1/2" x 2 1/4"
	Dark	6	3 1/2" x 3 1/2"
Unit B – Make 40 Dark	Background	1	2" x 3 3/4"
	Dark	2,3	2 1/4" x 3 1/2"
	Background	4,5	1 1/2" x 2 1/4"
	Medium	6	3 1/2" x 3 1/2"
Unit C – Make 20 ** No Paper	Background	1	6 1/2" x 6 1/2"
*Paper			7" x 7"

SEWING DIRECTIONS: 20 - 12" BLOCKS

1. Follow the position chart and sew all fabric onto units A and B. Make 10 blocks with the medium fabric and 10 blocks with the dark fabric. If using paper for the center pieces (unit C), assemble as well.

2. Trim the units leaving a 1/4" seam allowance.

3. Sew the units together following the diagram on how to assemble the block. Remove only the paper from the backside of the seam allowance; leave the remaining paper on until sewing the block to another block.

Make 10 Medium Blocks

Sew units A to units B. Make 20.

Sew units C to units AB. Make 10.

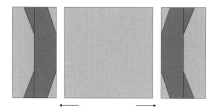

Sew together as shown

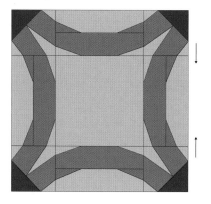

Make 10 Dark Blocks

Sew units A to units B. Make 20.

Sew units C to units AB. Make 10.

Sew together as shown

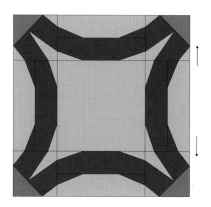

SEWING DIRECTIONS: OUTSIDE CURVED PIECES

1. Follow the position chart and sew all fabric onto units D, E and F. Make 9 outside curves with medium fabric and 9 outside curves with the dark fabric.

2. Trim the units leaving a 1/4" seam allowance.

3. Sew the units together following the diagram on how to assemble the curved block. Remove only the paper from the backside of the seam allowance; leave the remaining paper on until sewing the block to another block.

Make 9 Medium Curves

Sew units E and F to units D

Make 9 Dark Curves

Sew units G and H to units D

POSITION CHART:
OUTSIDE EDGE, 9 – MEDIUM, 9 – DARK

	Fabric	Position	Size
Unit D –	Background	1	2 1/2" x 7"
Make 9 Medium	Medium	2,3	1 1/2" x 3"
	Medium	4	2 1/4" x 7"
Unit D –	Background	1	2 1/2" x 7"
Make 9 Dark	Dark	2,3	1 1/2" x 3"
	Dark	4	2 1/4" x 7"
Units E & F –	Medium	1	2 1/2" x 3 1/4"
Make 9 each	Background	2	1 1/2" x 2 1/4"
Medium	Dark	3	2 1/4" x 2 1/2"
Units G & H –	Dark	1	2 1/2" x 3 1/4"
Make 9 each	Background	2	1 1/2" x 2 1/4"
Dark	Medium	3	2 1/4" x 2 1/2"

Solid Arc Wedding Ring

ASSEMBLING THE QUILT

1. Before assembling the quilt, it is very important sew (stay stitch) 1/8" on the curve of the outside pieces. This will help to stabilize the fabric when removing the paper.

2. Refer to the diagram and sew the outside curves to the blocks using a 1/4" seam allowance. Sew the blocks together in rows.

3. Remove the paper from the quilt, leaving the paper on the outside edges until the last. Be careful when removing this paper as not to stretch the outside edges.

4. Quilt as desired.

5. Trim off excess batting and backing.

6. Sew on bias binding.

"The Flower Ring" made by Carolyn Cullinan McCormick,
quilted by Carol Willey, Castle Rock, Colorado. Fabric by Timeless Treasures.

The Flower Ring

May 1940 · 24" x 24" Quilted · 1-16" Block

CUTTING INSTRUCTIONS

From the background fabric, cut:

✻ 1 – 3 1/2" x 36" strip. Cut the strip into 16 – 2 1/4" x 3 1/2" rectangles.

✻ 1 – 3 1/4" x 40" strip and 1 – 3 1/4" x 24" strip. Cut the strip into 32 – 2" x 3 1/4" rectangles.

✻ 1 – 3" x 24" strip. Cut the strip into 16 – 1 1/2" x 3" rectangles.

✻ 1 – 2 3/4" x 32" strip. Cut the strip into 16 – 2" x 2 3/4" rectangles

✻ 1 – 2 1/2" x 14" strip. Cut the strip into 8 – 1 3/4" x 2 1/2" rectangles.

✻ 1 – 2" x 32" strip. Cut the strip into 16 – 2" x 2" squares.

From the taupe fabric, cut:

✻ 1 – 3 1/2" x 7" strip. Cut the strip into 2 – 3 1/2" squares. Cut the squares into half-square triangles.

✻ 1 – 2 3/4" x 32" strip. Cut the strip into 16 – 2" x 2 3/4" rectangles.

✻ 1 – 2 1/2" x 40" strip. Cut the strip into 16 – 2" x 2 1/2" rectangles and 8 -1" x 2 1/2" rectangles.

From the medium fabric, cut:

✻ 1 – 3" x 36" strip. Cut the strip into 16 – 2 1/4" x 3" rectangles.

From the dark fabric, cut:

✻ 1 – 3 1/2" x 9" strip. Cut the strips into 4– 2 1/4" x 3 1/2" rectangles.

✻ 1 – 3 1/4" x 32" strip. Cut the strip into 16 – 2" x 3 1/4" rectangles.

✻ 1 – 3" x 32" strip. Cut the strip into 16 – 2" x 3" rectangles.

✻ 1 – 2 1/2" x 9" strip. Cut the strip into 4 – 2 1/4" x 2 1/2" rectangles.

✻ 1 – 1 3/4" x 15" strip. Cut the strip into 12 – 1 1/4" x 1 3/4" rectangles.

SUPPLY LIST

Make 4 copies of all units except unit H.
Make 16 copies of unit H.

FABRICS:

Background	5/8 yd.	
Taupe	3/8 yd.	
Medium		
Blocks	1/8 yd.	
Corner Triangles	1/2 yd.	
Total	5/8 yd.	
Dark		
Blocks	1/2 yd.	
Brown		
Blocks	1/4 yd.	
Border	1/4 yd.	
Binding	1/4 yd.	
Total	3/4 yd.	
Batting: 7/8 yd. 45" wide		
Backing: 7/8 yd.		

From the brown fabric, cut:

✻ 1 – 2" x 27" strip. Cut the strip into 4 – 2" x 6 3/4" rectangles.

✻ 1 – 2" x 22" strip. Cut the strip into 4 – 2" x 5 1/2" rectangles.

✻ 1 – 2" x 28" strip. Cut the strip into 8 – 2" x 3 1/2" rectangles.

CORNER TRIANGLES:

From the medium fabric, cut:

✻ 1 – 12 1/4" strip. Cut the strip into 2 – 12 1/4" squares. Cut the squares once on the diagonal.

BORDER AND BINDING:

From the brown fabric, cut:

Border:

✻ 4 – 1 1/2" strips.

Binding:

✻ 3 – 2 1/2" strips.

PATTERN ON PAGES 101–102.

The Flower Ring

POSITION CHART: I – 16" BLOCK

	Fabric	Position	Size
Unit A– Make 4	Dark	1	2 1/4" x 3 1/2"
	Background	2	1 3/4" x 2 1/2"
Units B & C – Make 4 Each	Background	1,3	2 1/4" x 3 1/2"
	Dark	2,4	2" x 3 1/4"
	Background	5	1 1/2" x 3"
	Brown	6	2" x 3 1/2"
Unit D – Make 4	Dark	1	2 1/4" x 2 1/2"
	Background	2	1 3/4" x 2 1/2"
Units E & F – Make 4 Each	Background	1,3	2" x 2 3/4"
	Dark	2,4	2" x 3"
	Background	5	1 1/2" x 3"
Unit G – Make 4	Dark	1,4,5	1 1/4" x 1 3/4"
	Background	2,3,6,7	2" x 2"
	Taupe	8,9	1" x 2 1/2"
	Taupe	10	3 1/2" x 3 1/2"
Unit H – Make 16	Taupe	1	2" x 2 1/2"
	Background	2,3	2" x 3 1/4"
Units I & J – Make 4 Each	Medium	1,3	2 1/4" x 3"
	Taupe	2,4	2" x 2 3/4"
Unit K – Make 4	Brown	1	2" x 5 1/2"
Unit L – Make 4	Brown	1	2" x 6 3/4"

SEWING DIRECTIONS: I– 16" BLOCK

1. Follow the position chart and sew all fabric onto the units.

2. Trim the units leaving a 1/4" seam allowance.

3. Sew the units together following the diagram on how to assemble the block. Press following the pressing arrows. Remove the paper from the backside of the seam allowance; leaving on the remaining paper.

Sew units B and C to units A.

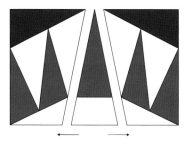

Sew units E and F to units D.

Sew units ABC to Units DEF. Make 4.

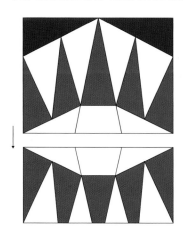

Sew units G together. Make 2

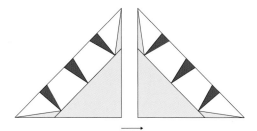

Sew the two units G together.

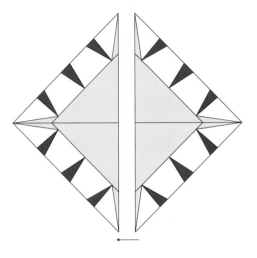

Sew units I to units J

Sew units H onto units IJ.

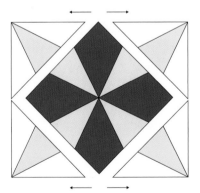

Sew units K to units HIJ.

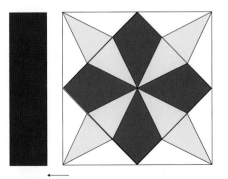

Sew units L to units HIJK. Make 4.

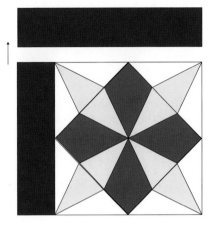

Follow the diagram and sew the block together.

The Flower Ring

ASSEMBLING THE QUILT

1. Refer to the diagram and sew on the corner triangles using a 1/4" seam allowance.

2. Remove the paper.

3. Add the border to the top and bottom of the quilt using 1/4" seam allowances. Press toward the border. Add the side borders and press the seam allowances toward the border.

4. Quilt as desired.

5. Trim off excess batting and backing.

6. Sew on binding.

"Rob Peter and Pay Paul" made by Carolyn Cullinan McCormick, quilted by Carol Willey, Castle Rock, Colorado.

Rob Peter and Pay Paul

October 1928 • 53" x 53" Quilted • 9 – 10" Dark Center Blocks • 4 – 10" Light Center Blocks

CUTTING INSTRUCTIONS

From the light fabric, cut:

* Paper

✳ 1 – 6 3/4" strip. Cut the strip into 4 – 6 3/4" squares.

** No Paper

✳ 1 – 6 3/8" strip. Cut the strip into 4 – 6 3/8" squares.

✳ 3 – 6 3/4" strips. Cut the strips into 36 – 3" x 6 3/4" rectangles.

✳ 1 – 4" strip. Cut the strip into 16 – 1 3/4" x 4" rectangles.

✳ 5- 3 3/4" strips. Cut the strips into 72 – 2 1/4" x 3 3/4" rectangles.

✳ 2 – 3 1/4" strips. Cut the strips into 32 – 1 1/2" x 3 1/4" rectangles.

From the dark fabric, cut:

* Paper

✳ 2 – 6 3/4" strips. Cut the strips into 9 – 6 3/4" squares.

**No Paper

✳ 2 – 6 3/8" strips. Cut the strips into 9 – 6 3/8" squares.

✳ 2 – 6 3/4" strips. Cut the strips into 16 – 3" x 6 3/4" rectangles.

✳ 2 – 4" strips. Cut the strips into 36 – 1 3/4" x 4" rectangles.

✳ 2 – 3 3/4" strips. Cut the strips into 32 – 2 1/4" x 3 3/4" rectangles.

✳ 3 – 3 1/4" strips. Cut the strips into 72 – 1 1/2" x 3 1/4" rectangles.

---

* ***** Paper – if using the paper template use this measurement.

* ****** No Paper – if not placing the fabric on the paper template that is provided use this measurement.

SUPPLY LIST

Units A & B – Make 36 Copies
Unit C – Make 9 Copies (If Using Paper)
Units D & E – Make 16 Copies
Unit F – Make 4 (If Using Paper)

FABRICS

Light		
Blocks	1 7/8 yds.	
2nd Border	3/8 yd.	
Total	2 1/4 yd.	

Dark		
Blocks	1 3/4 yds.	
Setting &		
Corner Triangles	3/4 yd.	
1st Border	3/8 yd.	
3rd Border	3/8 yd.	
Binding	1/2 yd.	
Total	3 3/4 yds.	

Batting: 1 3/4 yds. 90" wide
Backing: 3 1/2 yds.

SETTING AND CORNER TRIANGLES:

From the dark fabric, cut:

Setting Triangles

✳ 1 – 15 1/2" strip. Cut the strip into 2 – 15 1/2" squares. Cut the squares on the diagonal twice.

Corner Triangles

✳ 1 – 8" strip. Cut the strip into 2 – 8" squares. Cut the squares once on the diagonal.

PATTERN ON PAGE 103.

Rob Peter and Pay Paul

POSITION CHART:
9 – 10" DARK CENTER BLOCKS
4 – 10" LIGHT CENTER BLOCKS

	Fabric	Position	Size
Unit A – Make 36	Light	1	3" x 6 3/4"
	Dark	2,3	1 1/2" x 3 1/4"
Unit B – Make 36	Dark	1	1 3/4" x 4"
	Light	2,3	2 1/4" x 3 3/4"
Unit C – Make 9			
**No Paper	Dark	1	6 3/8" x 6 3/8"
* Paper			6 3/4" x 6 3/4"
Unit D – Make 16	Dark	1	3" x 6 3/4"
	Light	2,3	1 1/2" x 3 1/4"
Unit E – Make 16	Light	1	1 3/4" x 4"
	Dark	2,3	2 1/4" x 3 3/4"
Unit F – Make 4			
** No Paper	Light	1	6 3/8" x 6 3/8"
* Paper			6 3/4" x 6 3/4"

BORDERS AND BINDING:
From the dark fabric, cut:

1st Border
✳ 5 – 2 1/2" strips

3rd Border
✳ 5 – 2 1/2" strips

Binding
✳ 6 – 2 1/2" strips.

From the light fabric, cut:
2nd Border
✳ 5 – 2 1/2" strips

SEWING DIRECTIONS

1. Follow the position chart and sew all fabric onto units A, B, D and E. If using paper for the center pieces (units C and F), assemble as well.

2. Trim the units leaving a 1/4" seam allowance.

3. Sew the units together following the diagram on how to assemble the block. Remove only the paper from the backside of the seam allowance; leave the remaining paper on until sewing the block to another block.

Make 9 – Dark Center Blocks

Sew units A to units B

Sew units A to units C

Sew units AB to units AC

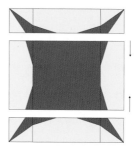

Make 4 – Light Center Blocks

Sew units D to units E

Sew units D to units F

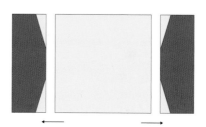

Sew units DE to units DF

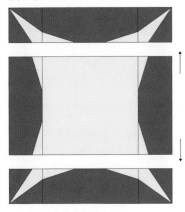

ASSEMBLING THE QUILT

1. Refer to the diagram and sew the rows of blocks, setting triangles and corner triangles together using a 1/4" seam allowance. Follow the arrows for pressing; this will help when sewing the rows together.

2. Remove the paper from the center of the quilt but do not remove the paper from the outside edges until the borders have been sewn on.

3. Add the first border to the top and bottom using 1/4" seam allowance. Press the seam allowances toward the border. Add the side borders then press the seams toward the border.

4. Remove the remaining paper.

5. Sew on the second and third borders following the same sequence as the first.

6. Quilt as desired.

7. Trim off excess batting and backing.

8. Sew on binding.

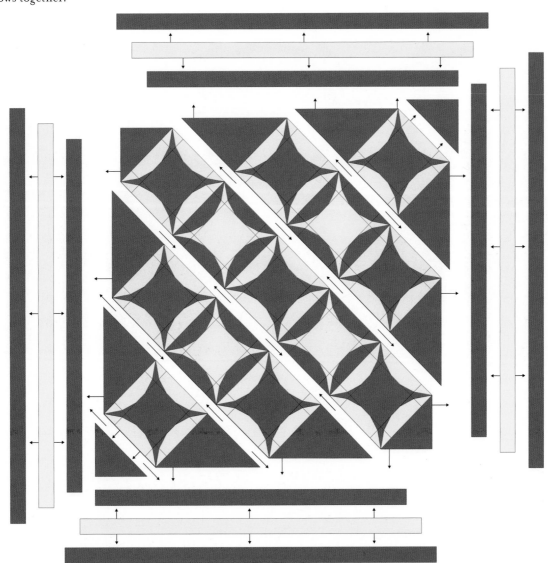

"The Broken Stone" made by Carolyn Cullinan McCormick,
quilted by Carol Willey, Castle Rock, Colorado.

The Broken Stone

September 1933 • 45" x 45" Quilted • 9 - 10" Blocks

CUTTING DIRECTIONS

From each of the 9 background fabrics or from the background yardage, cut:

✳ 1 – 5 1/4" x 21" strip. Cut the strip into 4 – 5 1/4" squares.

✳ 1 – 4 1/2" x 12" strip. Cut the strip into 8 – 1 1/2" x 4 1/2" rectangles.

✳ 1 – 4 1/2" x 9" strip. Cut the strip into 2 – 4 1/2" squares. Cut the squares into half-square triangles.

From each of the 9 dark fabrics or dark yardage, cut:

✳ 1 – 5 1/2" x 7" strip. Cut the strip into 4 – 1 3/4" x 5 1/2" rectangles.

✳ 1 – 4 3/4" x 7" strip. Cut the strip into 4 – 1 3/4" x 4 3/4" rectangles.

✳ 1 – 2 1/4" x 5" strip. Cut the strip into 4 – 1 1/4" x 2 1/4" rectangles.

Corner Triangles
From the dark fabric, cut:

✳ 2 – 22 7/8" strips. Cut the strips into 2 – 22 7/8" squares. Cut the squares once on the diagonal.

Binding:
From the dark fabric, cut:

✳ 5 – 2 1/2" strips.

Borders:
From the red fabric, cut:

✳ 1st border: 4 – 1" strips

✳ 2nd border: 5 – 1 1/2" strips

PATTERN ON PAGE 107.

PATTERN ON PAGE 107.

SUPPLY LIST

Unit A – Make 36 Copies

FABRICS:

Background	9 Fat Quarters (For a scrappy look) 1 3/4 yds. if using one fabric
Dark	
Blocks	9 Fat Quarters (For a scrappy look) 7/8 yds. if using one fabric
Corner Triangles	1 3/8 yds.
Binding	1/2 yd.
Red	
Borders	3/8 yd.

Batting: 1 3/8 yds. 90" wide
Backing: 3 yds.

The Broken Stone

POSITION CHART: 9 – 10" BLOCKS

	Fabric	Position	Size
Unit A – Make 36	Background	1	5 1/4" x 5 1/4"
	Dark	2	1 1/4" x 2 1/4"
	Dark	3	1 3/4" x 4 3/4"
	Dark	4	1 3/4" x 5 1/2"
	Background	5,6	1 1/2" x 4 1/2"
	Background	7	4 1/2" x 4 1/2"

SEWING DIRECTIONS: 9 – 10" BLOCKS

1. Follow the position chart and sew all fabric onto units A.

2. Trim the units leaving a 1/4" seam allowance.

3. Sew the units together following the diagram on how to assemble the block. Remove only the paper from the backside of the seam allowance; leave the remaining paper on until sewing the block to another block.

Sew units A together.
Press all one direction.

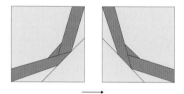

Sew together as shown.

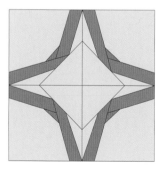

ASSEMBLING THE QUILT

1. Refer to the diagram and sew the rows of blocks together using 1/4" seam allowance. Follow the arrows for pressing; this will help when sewing the rows together.

2. Remove the paper from the center of the quilt but do not remove the paper from the outside edges.

3. Add the first border to the top and bottom using 1/4" seam allowance. Press toward the border. Add the side borders and press the seam allowances toward the border.

4. Remove the remaining paper.

5. Add the corner triangles using 1/4" seam allowance. Press toward the corner triangles.

6. Add the second border to the top and bottom using 1/4" seam allowance. Press toward the border. Add the side borders and press the seam allowances toward the border.

7. Quilt as desired.

8. Trim off excess batting and backing.

9. Sew on binding.

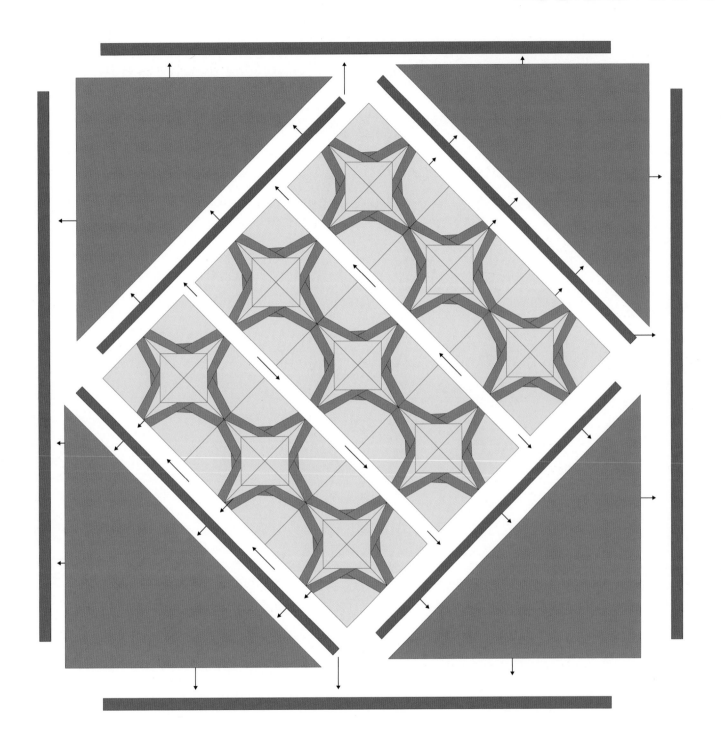

"Jake" (The Broken Stone) *made by Carolyn Cullinan McCormick, quilted by Carol Willey, Castle Rock, Colorado.*

"Jake" (The Broken Stone)

January 1950 • 59" x 73" Quilted • 18 - 10" Blocks

CUTTING INSTRUCTIONS

From the light fabric, cut:

✳ 11 – 4 3/4" strips. Cut the strips into 82 – 4 3/4" squares.

From the dark green fabric, cut:

✳ 8 – 3" strips. Cut the strips into 164 – 1 3/4" x 3" rectangles.

✳ 4 – 6 1/4" strips. Cut the strips into 82 – 1 3/4" x 6 1/4" rectangles.

From the brown fabric, cut:

✳ 4 – 3 1/2" strips. Cut the strips into 46 – 3 1/2" squares. Cut the squares into half-square triangles.

From the print fabric, cut: (Select One Method)

*Paper

3 – 6 1/4" strips. Cut strips into 18 – 6 1/4" squares.

**No Paper

3 – 5 3/4" strips. Cut the strips into 18 – 5 3/4" squares.

***Fussy Cut – 18 — 5 1/4" squares for the blocks and 4 for cornerstones. Refer to page 4 for directions on How to Fussy Cut Squares.

SETTING AND CORNER TRIANGLES:

From the light fabric, cut:

Pieced Setting Triangles

✳ 5 – 3 1/4" strips. Cut the strips into 10 – 3 1/4" x 15 3/8" rectangles. Cut the rectangles on both ends on the 45° angle.

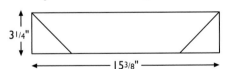

3 1/4"   15 3/8"

Corner Triangles

✳ 1 – 8" strip. Cut the strip into 2 - 8" squares. Cut the squares on the diagonal.

> * Paper – if using the paper template use this measurement.
>
> ** No Paper – if not placing the fabric on the paper template that is provided use this measurement.

SUPPLY LIST

Unit A – Make 46 Copies
Unit B – Make 36 Copies
Unit C –Make 18 copies (If using Paper)

FABRICS:

Light	
Blocks	1 5/8 yds.
Setting & Corner	
Triangles	3/4 yd.
Total	2 3/8 yds.
Dark	
Blocks	1 1/2 yds.
2nd Border	1 yd.
Total	2 1/2 yds.
Brown	
Blocks	1/2 yd.
1st Border	1/2 yd.
3rd Border	5/8 yd.
Binding	5/8 yd.
Total	2 1/4 yds.
Print	3/4 yd.

If you want to "fussy cut" art elements from your fabric, purchase enough to have 18 pieces for the blocks and 4 for the cornerstones.

Batting: 1 7/8 yd. 90" wide

Backing: 4 1/2 yds.

BORDERS AND BINDING:

From the brown fabric, cut:

1st border

✳ 6 – 2 1/2" strips.

3rd border

✳ 7 – 2 1/2" strips.

Binding

✳ 7 – 2 1/2" strips.

From the dark green fabric, cut:

2nd border

✳ 6 – 5 3/4" strips.

From the print fabric, cut:

Cornerstones

✳ 4 – 5 3/4" squares. Fussy cut if you wish.

PATTERN ON PAGES 108–109.

"Jake" (The Broken Stone)

POSITION CHART: 18 – 10" BLOCKS

	Fabric	Position	Size
Unit A – Make 46	Light	1	4 3/4" x 4 3/4"
	Dark Green	2,3	1 3/4" x 3"
	Dark Green	4	1 3/4" x 6 1/4"
	Brown	5,6	3 1/2" x 3 1/2"
Unit B – Make 36	Light	1	4 3/4" x 4 3/4"
	Dark Green	2,3	1 3/4" x 3"
	Dark Green	4	1 3/4" x 6 1/4"
Unit C – Make 18			
*Paper	Print	1	6 1/4" x 6 1/4"
** No Paper			5 3/4" x 5 3/4"
*** Fussy Cut			See Directions

*   Paper – if using the paper template, use this measurement.
** No Paper – if not placing the fabric on the paper template
     that is provided, use this measurement.
*** Fussy Cut – See cutting directions.

SEWING DIRECTIONS

1. Follow the position chart and sew all fabric onto the units A and B. If using paper for the center piece (unit C) assemble as well.

2. Trim the units leaving a 1/4" seam allowance.

3. Sew units together following the diagram on how to assemble the block. Remove only the paper from the backside of the seam allowance; leave the remaining paper on until sewing the block to another block.

   Sew units B to units C
   Press to the center.

Sew units A to units BC

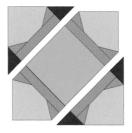

4. Sew units together making 18 blocks.

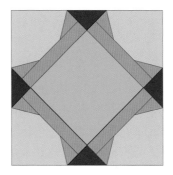

5. Follow the diagram to make the pieced setting triangles. Sew a unit A to the short side of each rectangle. Press to the solid side. Make 10.

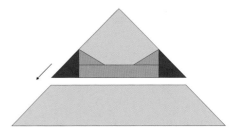

ASSEMBLING THE QUILT

1. Refer to the diagram and sew the rows of blocks, setting triangles and corner triangles together using 1/4" seam allowance. Follow the arrows for pressing; this will help when sewing the rows together.

2. Remove the paper from the center of the quilt but do not remove the paper from the outside edges until the borders have been sewn on.

3. Add the first border to the top and bottom using 1/4" seam allowances. Press toward the border. Add the side borders and press the seam allowances toward the border.

4. Remove the remaining paper.

5. Sew the second border on the top and bottom. Add the cornerstones to each side piece then sew a border on to each side.

6. Add the third border.

7. Quilt as desired.

8. Trim off excess batting and backing.

9. Sew on binding.

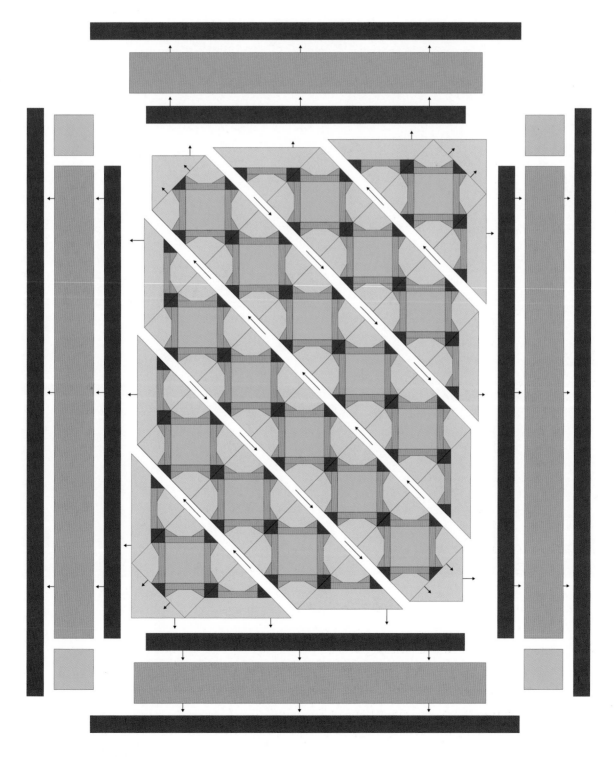

"Hands all 'Round" made by Carolyn Cullinan McCormick,
quilted by Carol Willey, Castle Rock, Colorado.

Hands all 'Round

August 1929 • 42" x 42" Quilted • 13 - 10" Blocks

CUTTING INSTRUCTIONS

From the light fabric, cut:

❋ 5 – 3 1/2" strips. Cut the strips into 52 – 3 1/2" squares. Cut the squares into half-square triangles.

❋ 8 – 2 3/4" strips. Cut the strips into 104 – 2 3/4" squares.

From the medium fabric, cut:

❋ 3 – 7" strips. Cut the strips into 52 – 2" x 7" rectangles.

❋ 5 – 3 1/2" strips. Cut the strips into 52 – 3 1/2" squares. Cut the squares into half-square triangles.

❋ 5 – 2 3/4" strips. Cut the strips into 52 – 1 1/2" x 2 3/4" rectangles, 52 – 1 1/4" x 2 3/4" rectangles and 13 – 2 3/4" x 2 3/4" squares.

❋ 4 – 1 3/4" strips. Cut the strips into 104 – 1 1/4" x 1 3/4" rectangles.

From the dark fabric, cut:

❋ 4 – 3" strips. Cut the strips into 52 - 2 3/4" x 3" rectangles.

❋ 7 – 2 1/2" strips. Cut the strips into 104 – 2 1/2" squares.

SETTING AND CORNER TRIANGLES:

From the dark fabric, cut:

Setting Triangles:

❋ 1 – 15 1/2" strip. Cut the strip into 2 – 15 1/2" squares. Cut the squares on the diagonal twice.

Corner Triangles:

❋ 1 – 8" strip. Cut the strip into 2 – 8" squares. Cut the squares once on the diagonal.

BINDING:

From the medium fabric, cut:

5 – 2 1/2" strips.

SUPPLY LIST

Unit A – Make 52 Copies
Unit B – Make 52 Copies
Unit C – Make 39 Copies
Unit D – Make 13 Copies

FABRICS:

Light	
Blocks	1 1/4 yds.
Medium	
Blocks	1 3/4 yds.
Binding	1/2 yd.
Total	2 1/4 yds.
Dark	
Blocks	1 yd.
Setting &	
Corner Triangles	3/4 yd.
Total	1 3/4 yds.
Batting: 49" x 49"	
Backing: 2 3/4 yds.	

PATTERN ON PAGE 110.

Hands all 'Round

POSITION CHART: 13 – 10" BLOCKS

	Fabric	Position	Size
Unit A – Make 52	Light	1	2 3/4" x 2 3/4"
	Medium	2,3	3 1/2" x 3 1/2" ◣
	Light	4,5	3 1/2" x 3 1/2" ◣
	Medium	6	2" x 7"
Unit B – Make 52	Medium	1	1 1/2" x 2 3/4"
	Dark	2,3	2 1/2" x 2 1/2"
Unit C – Make 39	Light	1	2 3/4" x 2 3/4"
	Dark	2	2 3/4" x 3"
	Medium	3,4	1 1/4" x 1 3/4"
	Medium	5	1 1/4" x 2 3/4"
Unit D – Make 13	Light	1	2 3/4" x 2 3/4"
	Dark	2	2 3/4" x 3"
	Medium	3,4	1 1/4" x 1 3/4"
	Medium	5	1 1/4" x 2 3/4"
	Medium	6	2 3/4" x 2 3/4"

Sew units AB to units C.

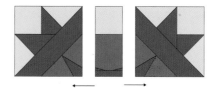

Sew units together as shown.

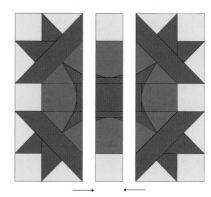

SEWING DIRECTIONS: 13 – 10" BLOCKS

1. Follow the position chart and sew all fabric onto the units.

2. Trim the units leaving a 1/4" seam allowance.

3. Sew the units together following the diagram on how to assemble the block. Press following the pressing arrows. Remove only the paper from the backside of the seam allowance; leave the remaining paper on until sewing the block to another block.

Sew units A to units B

Sew units C to units D.

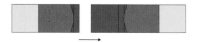

ASSEMBLING THE QUILT

1. Refer to the diagram and sew the rows of blocks, setting triangles and corner triangles together using 1/4" seam allowance. Follow the arrows for pressing; this will help when sewing the rows together.

2. Remove the paper.

3. Quilt as desired.

4. Trim off excess batting and backing.

5. Sew on binding.

"Lafayette Orange Peel" made by Carolyn Cullinan McCormick,
quilted by Carol Willey, Castle Rock, Colorado. Fabric by Batik Textiles.

Lafayette Orange Peel

April 1929 • 36 1/2" x 36 1/2" Quilted • 5-10" Blocks

CUTTING INSTRUCTIONS

From the light fabric, cut:

✳ 2 – 6" strips. Cut the strips into 40 – 2" x 6" rectangles.

✳ 2 – 5 1/2" strips. Cut the strips into 40 – 2" x 5 1/2" rectangles.

✳ 2 – 3 1/2" strips. Cut the strips into 40 – 1 1/2" x 3 1/2" rectangles.

✳ 2 – 2 3/4" strips. Cut the strips into 40 – 1 1/4" x 2 3/4" rectangles.

From the dark fabric, cut:

✳ 3 – 8 1/4" strips. Cut the strips into 20 – 4 1/4" x 8 1/4" rectangles.

SETTING AND CORNER TRIANGLES:

From the dark fabric, cut:

✳ 1 – 15 1/2" strip. Cut the strip into 1 – 15 1/2" square. Cut the square on the diagonal twice.

✳ 1 – 8" strip. Cut the strip into 2 – 8" squares. Cut the squares once on the diagonal.

SUPPLY LIST

Unit A – Make 20 Copies

FABRICS:

Light	
Blocks	1 1/8 yds.
1st Border	1/4 yd.
Binding	3/8 yd.
Total	1 3/4 yds.
Dark	
Blocks	3/4 yd.
Setting & Corner Triangles	3/4 yd.
2nd Border	1/2 yd.
Total	2 yds.
Batting: 43" x 43"	
Backing: 1 1/4 yds.	

BORDERS AND BINDING:

From the light fabric, cut:

1st Border:

✳ 4 - 1 1/2" strips.

Binding:

✳ 4 – 2 1/2" strips.

From the dark fabric, cut:

2nd Border:

✳ 4 – 4" strips.

PATTERN ON PAGE III.

Lafayette Orange Peel

POSITION CHART: 5 -10" BLOCKS

	Fabric	Position	Size
Unit A – Make 20	Dark	1	4 1/4" x 8 1/4"
	Light	2,3	1 1/4" x 2 3/4"
	Light	4,5	1 1/2" x 3 1/2"
	Light	6,7	2" x 5 1/2"
	Light	8,9	2" x 6"

SEWING DIRECTIONS

1. Follow the position chart and sew all fabric onto units A.

2. Trim the units, leaving a 1/4" seam allowance.

3. Sew the units together following the diagram on how to assemble the block. Remove only the paper from the backside of the seam allowance; leave the remaining paper on until sewing the block to another block.

Sew units A together.
Press all one direction.

Sew together as shown.

ASSEMBLING THE QUILT

1. Refer to the diagram and sew the rows of blocks, setting triangles and corner triangles together using 1/4" seam allowance. Follow the arrows for pressing; this will help when sewing the rows together.

2. Remove the paper from the center of the quilt but do not remove the paper from the outside edges until the borders have been sewn on.

3. Add the first border to the top and bottom using 1/4" seam allowance. Press towards the border. Add the side borders and press the seam allowances toward the border.

4. Remove the remaining paper.

5. Sew the second border following the same sequence.

6. Quilt as desired.

7. Trim off excess batting and backing.

8. Sew on binding.

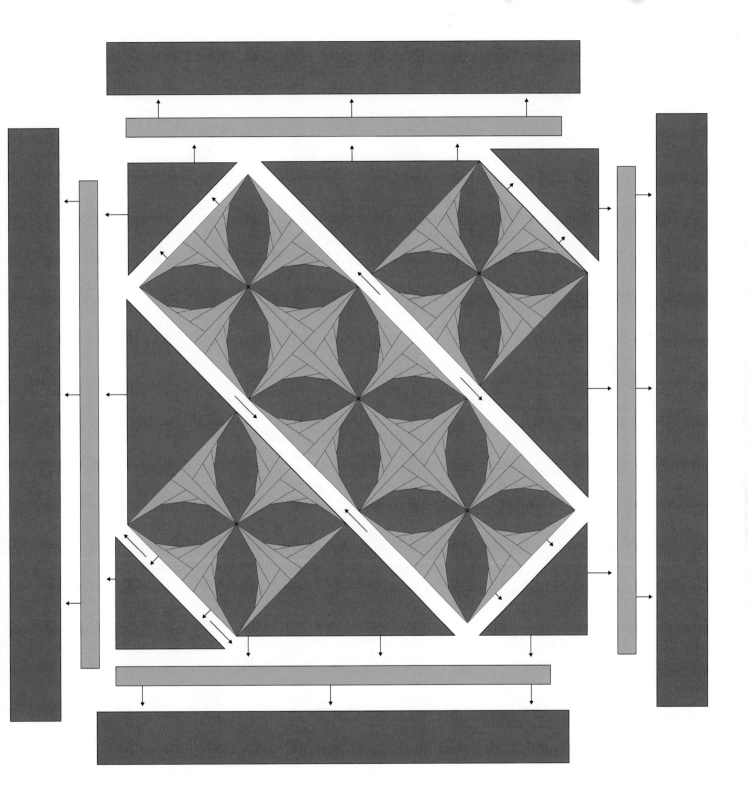

"Interlocking Wedding Rings" made by Carolyn Cullinan McCormick, quilted by Carol Willey, Castle Rock, Colorado.

Interlocked Wedding Rings

CUTTING INSTRUCTIONS

From the background fabric, cut:

* Paper

✳ 5 – 7" strips. Cut the strips into 30 – 7" squares.

** No Paper

✳ 5 – 6 1/2" strips. Cut the strips into 30 – 6 1/2" squares.

✳ 13 – 3 3/4" strips. Cut the strips into 284 – 1 3/4" x 3 3/4" rectangles.

✳ 5 – 2" strips. Cut the strips into 84 – 2" squares. Cut the squares into half-square triangles.

From the dark fabric, cut:

✳ 5 – 7" strips. Cut the strips into 71 – 2 1/2" x 7" rectangles.

✳ 4 – 3 3/4" strips. Cut the strips into 71 – 1 3/4" x 3 3/4" rectangles.

✳ 6 – 3 1/4" strips. Cut the strips into 84 – 2 1/2" x 3 1/4" rectangles.

From the print fabric, cut:

✳ 5 – 7" strips. Cut the strips into 71 – 2 1/2" x 7" rectangles.

✳ 4 – 3 3/4" strips. Cut the strips into 71 – 1 3/4" x 3 3/4" rectangles.

✳ 6 – 3 1/4" strips. Cut the strips into 84 – 2 1/2" x 3 1/4" rectangles.

BORDERS AND BINDING:

From the dark fabric, cut:

First border

✳ 6 – 2 1/2" strips.

Binding

✳ 7 – 2 1/2" strips.

SUPPLY LIST

Units A & B – Make 71 Copies
Units C & D – Make 42 Copies
Unit E – Make 30 (If using Paper)

FABRIC:		
Background	2 3/4 yd.	
Dark		
Blocks	2 1/8 yd.	
1st Border	1/2 yd.	
Binding	5/8 yd.	
Total	3 1/4 yds.	
Print		
Blocks	2 1/8 yds.	
2nd Border	1 1/8 yds.	
Total	3 1/4 yds.	

Batting: 2 yds. 90" wide
Backing: 4 1/4 yds.

From the print fabric, cut:

2nd border

✳ 7 – 5" strips.

---

*   Paper – if using the paper template use this measurement.

** No Paper – if not placing the fabric on the paper template that is provided use this measurement.

PATTERN ON PAGES 112–113.

Interlocked Wedding Rings

POSITION CHART

	Fabric	Position	Size
Unit A – Make 71	Print	1	2 1/2" x 7"
	Background	2,3	1 3/4" x 3 3/4"
	Dark	4	1 3/4" x 3 3/4"
Unit B – Make 71	Dark	1	2 1/2" x 7"
	Background	2,3	1 3/4" x 3 3/4"
	Print	4	1 3/4" x 3 3/4"
Units C & D	Dark	1	2 1/2" x 3 1/4"
Make 42 each	Background	2,4	2" x 2"
	Print	3	2 1/2" x 3 1/4"
Unit E – Make 30			
** No Paper	Background	1	6 1/2" x 6 1/2"
*Paper			7" x 7"

SEWING DIRECTIONS

1. Follow the position chart and sew all fabric onto units A, B, C and D. If using paper for the center pieces (unit E), assemble as well.

2. Trim the units leaving a 1/4" seam allowance.

3. Sew the units together following the diagrams. Remove only the paper from the backside of the seam allowances; leave the remaining paper on until sewing the rows together.

Sew units A to units B

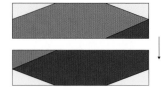

Sew units C to units D

4. Follow the diagrams carefully and sew the units together in rows. Remove only the paper from the backside of the seam allowance; leave the remaining paper on until sewing the rows together.

Row A - Make 4

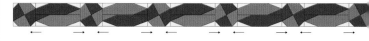

Row B - Make 3

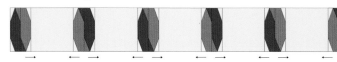

Row C - Make 3

Row D - Make 3

ASSEMBLING THE QUILT

1. Refer to the diagram and sew the rows together using 1/4" seam allowance. Carefully check to make sure you have the correct row before sewing.

2. Remove the paper from the center of the quilt but do not remove the paper from the outside edges until the borders have been sewn on.

3. Add the first border to the top and bottom using 1/4" seam allowance. Press toward the border. Add the side borders and press the seam allowances toward the border.

4. Sew on the second border following the same sequence as the first.

5. Remove the remaining paper.

6. Quilt as desired.

7. Trim off excess batting and backing.

8. Sew on binding.

Interlocked Wedding Rings

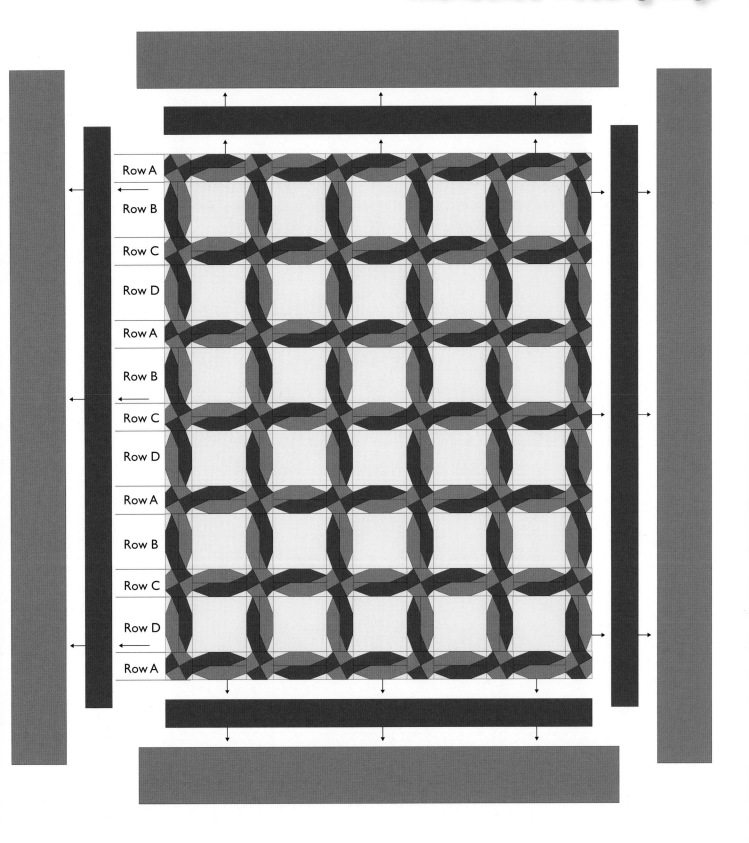

Row A
Row B
Row C
Row D
Row A
Row B
Row C
Row D
Row A
Row B
Row C
Row D
Row A

"Four Leaf Clover" made by Carolyn Cullinan McCormick, quilted by Carol Willey, Castle Rock, Colorado. Fabric by Batik Textiles.

Four Leaf Clover

September 1935 · 38" x 52 1/2" Quilted · 8-10" Blocks

CUTTING INSTRUCTIONS

From the background fabric, cut:

❋ 3 – 7" strips. Cut the strips into 32 – 3" x 7" rectangles.

❋ 4 – 3 1/2" strips. Cut the strips into 64 – 2" x 3 1/2" rectangles.

* Paper

❋ 1 – 3" strip. Cut the strip into 8 – 3" squares.

** No Paper

❋ 1 – 2 1/2" strip. Do not cut into squares.

From the black fabric, cut:

* Paper

❋ 3 – 3" strips. Cut the strips into 32 – 3" squares.

** No Paper

❋ 3 – 2 1/2" strips. Do not cut into squares.

From the print fabric, cut:

❋ 2 – 4" strips. Cut the strips into 32 - 2" x 4" rectangles.

❋ 3 – 3 1/4" strips. Cut the strips into 64 –1 3/4" x 3 1/4" rectangles.

* Paper

❋ 3 – 3" strips. Cut the strips into 32 – 3" squares.

** No Paper

❋ 2 – 2 1/2" strips. Do not cut into squares.

SETTING AND CORNER TRIANGLES:

From the print fabric, cut:

❋ 1 – 15 1/2" strip. Cut the strip into 2 – 15 1/2" squares. Cut the squares on the diagonal twice. Six setting triangles are needed.

❋ 1 – 8" strip. Cut the strip into 2 – 8" squares. Cut the squares once on the diagonal.

SUPPLY LIST

Unit A – Make 32 Copies
Unit B – Make 32 Copies
Units C, D and E – Make 8 Copies
   (If using *Paper)

FABRICS:

Background	1 1/4 yd.	
Black		
Blocks	3/8 yd.	
Binding	1/2 yd.	
1st Border	3/8 yd.	
Total	1 1/4 yds.	
Print		
Blocks	7/8 yd.	
Setting & Corner		
Triangles	3/4 yd.	
2nd Border	5/8 yd.	
Total	2 1/4 yds.	
Batting:	1 3/4 yds.	
Backing:	1 3/4 yds.	44" wide

BORDERS AND BINDING:

From the black fabric, cut:
1st border:

❋ 4 – 2 1/2" strips

Binding:

❋ 5 – 2 1/2" strips.

From the print fabric, cut:
2nd Border:

5 – 4" strips.

> *   Paper – if using the paper template use this measurement.
>
> ** No Paper – if not placing the fabric on the paper template that is provided use this measurement.

PATTERN ON PAGES 114–115.

Four Leaf Clover

POSITION CHART: 8 – 10" BLOCKS

	Fabric	Position	Size
Unit A – Make 32	Background	1	3" x 7"
	Print	2,3	1 3/4" x 3 1/4"
Unit B – Make 32	Print	1	2" x 4"
	Background	2,3	2" x 3 1/2"
Units C & E			
Make 8 Each			
*Paper	Print	1,3	3" x 3"
	Black	2	3" x 3"
** No Paper			
Unit D – Make 8			
*Paper	Black	1,3	3" x 3"
	Background	2	3" x 3"
** No Paper			

** No Paper – Follow cutting and sewing directions.

SEWING DIRECTIONS

1. This block will be sewn together differently. You will make and sew strip sets together for the center of the block. When making strip sets, sew the first two pieces from the top down. When adding the second piece, start from the bottom up. This technique will help eliminate curves in the strip set.

   There is also the option to sew the fabrics on the paper. Use the option you prefer.

   Make one strip set using the following fabrics cut 2 1/2" wide. Sew with a scant 1/4" seam allowance. Press toward the black.

   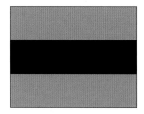

   Make one strip set using the following fabrics cut 2 1/2" wide. Sew with a scant 1/4" seam allowance. Press toward the black.

2. Cut the strip sets into 2 1/2" pieces. You will need 16 print / black/print combinations and 8 black/background/ black combinations.

   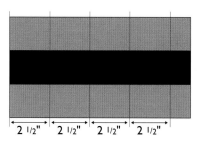

3. Follow the chart and sew the strip sets together. Make 8.

   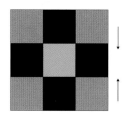

4. Follow the position chart and sew all fabric on to units A and B and C, D and E if you wish to paper piece these units.

5. Trim the units, leaving a 1/4" seam allowance.

6. Sew the units together following the assembly diagram. Press following the arrows. Remove only the paper from the back of the seam allowance; leave the remaining paper on until sewing the blocks together.

   Sew units A to center of block. Make 8

   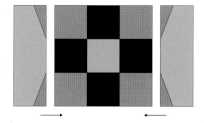

   Sew units A to units B. Make 16.

Four Leaf Clover

Sew together as shown.

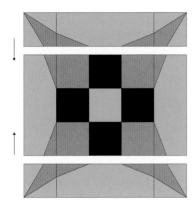

ASSEMBLING THE QUILT

1. Refer to the diagram and sew the rows of blocks, setting triangles and corner triangles together using a 1/4" seam allowance. Follow the arrows for pressing, this will help when sewing the rows together.

2. Remove the paper from the center of the quilt.

3. Add the first border to the top and bottom using 1/4" seam allowances. Press toward the border. Add the side borders and press the seam allowances toward the border.

4. Sew the second border following the same sequence.

5. Quilt as desired.

6. Trim off excess batting and backing.

7. Sew on the binding.

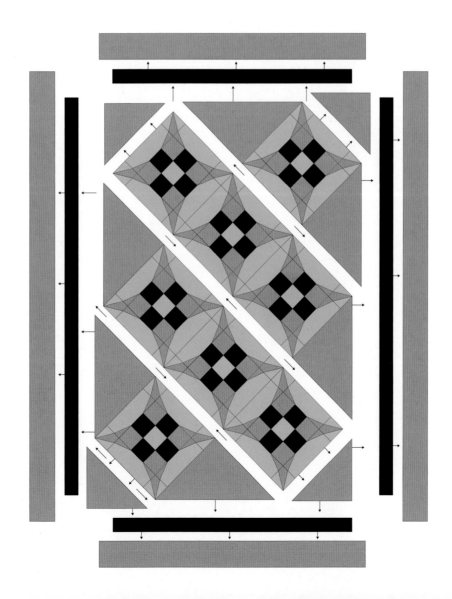

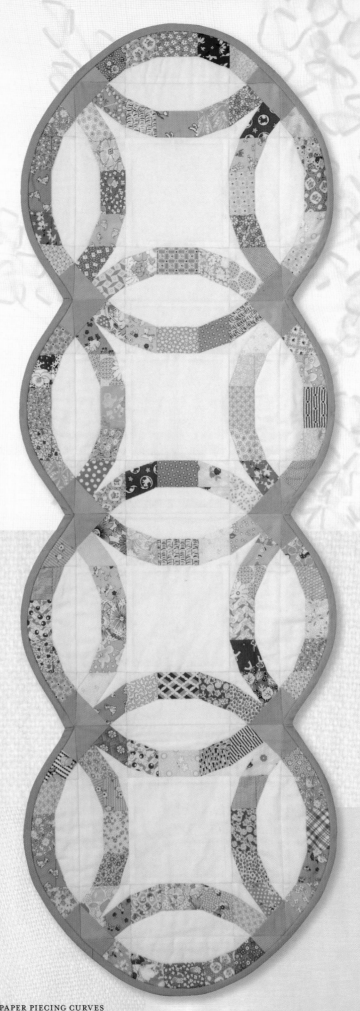

*"Wedding Ring Table Runner" made and
quilted by Carolyn Cullinan McCormick*

Wedding Ring Table Runner

4 – 10" Blocks • 15" x 44 1/2" Quilted • 10 – Outside Curved Blocks

CUTTING INSTRUCTIONS

From the background fabric, cut:

* Paper

✳ 1 – 6" x 24" strip. Cut the strip into 4 – 6" squares.

** No Paper

✳ 1 – 5 1/2" x 22" strip. Cut the strip into 4 – 5 ½" squares.

✳ 1 – 6" x 38 1/4" strip and 1 – 6" x 20 1/4" strip. Cut the strips into 26 – 2 1/4" x 6" rectangles.

✳ 1 – 3 1/4" x 24" strip. Cut the strip into 16 – 1 1/2" x 3 1/4" rectangles.

✳ 1 – 2 1/2" x 39" strip and 1 – 2 1/2" x 9" strip. Cut the strips into 32 – 1 1/2" x 2 1/2" rectangles.

✳ 1 – 2" x 38" strip and 1 – 2" x 30" strip. Cut the strips into 10 – 2" x 2" squares. Cut the squares into half-square triangles. Cut 32 – 1 1/2" x 2" rectangles.

From various scrap fabrics, cut:

✳ 52 – 2" x 3" rectangles.

✳ 26 – 2 1/4" x 2 3/4" rectangles.

✳ 52 – 2 1/4" x 2 1/2" rectangles. These pieces must match with units B & G. (See sewing units together.)

✳ 52 – 1 1/2" x 2 1/2" rectangles. These pieces must match with units A & F. (See sewing units together.)

From the green fabric, cut:

✳ 1 – 3" x 12" strip. Cut the strip into 4 – 3" squares. Cut the squares into 8 half-square triangles.

✳ 1 – 2 3/4" x 13 3/4" strip. Cut the strip into 5 – 2 3/4" squares. Cut the squares into 10 half-square triangles.

SUPPLY LIST	
Units A & B – Make 16 Copies	
Units C & D – Make 8 Copies	
Unit E – Make 4 Copies (If using Paper)	
Units F & G – Make 10 Copies	
Units H & I – Make 8 Copies	
Units J & K – Make 2 Copies	
FABRICS:	
Background	1 yd.
Print	Various Scraps
Pink	Fat Eighth
Green	Fat Eighth
Bias Binding	
Green	1/2 yd.
Backing: 20" x 49"	
Batting: 20" x 49"	

From the pink fabric, cut:

✳ 1 – 3" x 12" strip. Cut the strip into 4 – 3" squares. Cut the squares into 8 half-square triangles.

✳ 1 – 2 3/4" x 13 3/4" strip. Cut the strip into 5 – 2 3/4" squares. Cut the squares into 10 half-square triangles.

From the green fabric, cut:

✳ 132" of 2 1/2" bias binding.

---

* Paper – if using the paper template use this measurement.

** No Paper – if not placing the fabric on the paper template that is provided use this measurement.

PATTERN ON PAGES 116 – 118.

Wedding Ring Table Runner

POSITION CHART: 4 - 10" BLOCKS

	Fabric	Position	Size
Unit A – Make 16	Print	1	2 1/4" x 2 3/4"
	***Print	2,3	2 1/4" x 2 1/2"
	Background	4,5	1 1/2" x 2 1/2"
Unit B –Make 16	Background	1	2 1/4" x 6"
	***Print	2,3	1 1/2" x 2 1/2"
Unit C – Make 8	Background	1	1 1/2" x 3 1/4"
	Print	2,3	2" x 3"
	Background	4,5	1 1/2" x 2"
	Green	6	3" x 3"
Unit D - Make 8	Background	1	1 1/2" x 3 1/4"
	Print	2,3	2" x 3"
	Background	4,5	1 1/2" x 2"
	Pink	6	3" x 3"
Unit E –Make 4			
** No Paper	Background	1	5 1/2" x 5 1/2"
* Paper			6" x 6"

*** It is very important to remember when sewing the fabrics onto units B2 and B3 that they must correspond with the fabrics on units A2 and A3.

SEWING DIRECTIONS: BLOCKS

1. Follow the position chart and sew all fabric onto units A, B, C and D. If using paper for the center pieces (unit E), assemble as well.

2. It is very important to remember when sewing the fabrics onto units B2 and B3 that they must correspond with the fabrics on units A2 and A3.

3. Trim the units leaving 1/4" seam allowance.

4. Sew the units together following the diagram on how to assemble the block. Remove only the paper from the backside of the seam allowance; leave the remaining paper on until sewing the block to another block.

Sew units A to units B

Make 2 – #1 blocks. **Note:** #1 and #2 blocks are all made using the same units. The only difference is the way they are pressed. Each block is pressed differently to make it easier for you to join the blocks together.

Sew units C and D to each side of units AB. Make 4 following these pressing arrows.

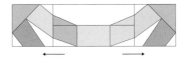

Sew units AB to each side of units E

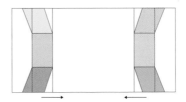

Sew together as shown

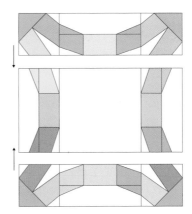

Make 2 – #2 blocks
Sew units C and D to each side of units AB
Make 4 following these pressing arrows.

Sew units AB to each side of units E

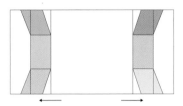

Sew together as shown.

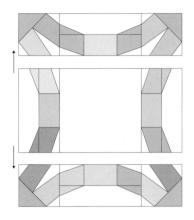

SEWING DIRECTIONS: OUTSIDE CURVED PIECES

1. Follow the position chart and sew all fabric onto units F, G, H, I, J and K.

2. It is very important to remember when sewing the fabrics onto units G2 and G3 that they must correspond with the fabrics on units F2 and F3.

3. Trim the units leaving 1/4" seam allowance.

4. Sew the units together following the diagram on how to assemble the curved block. Remove only the paper from the backside of the seam allowance; leave the remaining paper on until sewing the block to another block.

Make 10 - FGHI Outside Curves

Sew units F to units G

POSITION CHART: OUTSIDE CURVES, 10 CURVES

	Fabric	Position	Size	
Unit F – Make 10	Print	1	2 1/4" x 2 3/4"	
	***Print	2,3	2 1/4" x 2 1/2"	
Unit G –Make 10	Background	1	2 1/4" x 6"	
	***Print	2,3	1 1/2" x 2 1/2"	
Unit H – Make 8	Print	1	2" x 3"	
	Background	2	2" x 2"	◪
	Pink	3	2 3/4" x 2 3/4"	◪
Unit I – Make 8	Print	1	2" x 3"	
	Background	2	2" x 2"	◪
	Green	3	2 3/4" x 2 3/4"	◪
Unit J –Make 2	Print	1	2" x 3"	
	Background	2	2" x 2"	◪
	Pink	3	2 3/4" x 2 3/4"	◪
Unit K – Make 2	Print	1	2" x 3"	
	Background	2	2" x 2"	◪
	Green	3	2 3/4" x 2 3/4"	◪

***It is very important to remember when sewing the fabrics onto units G2 and G3 that they must correspond with the fabrics on units F2 and F3.

Sew units H and I to units FG
Make 4 - #3 blocks pressing as following.

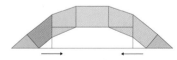

Make 4 - #4 blocks pressing as following.

Wedding Ring Table Runner

Sew units J and K to units FD
Make 1 - #5 block pressing as following.

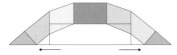

Make 1 - #6 block pressing as following.

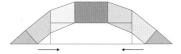

ASSEMBLING THE QUILT

1. Before assembling the quilt, it is very important to sew (stay stitch) 1/8" on the curve of the outside pieces. This will help to stabilize the fabric when removing the paper.

2. Refer to the diagram and sew the outside curves to the blocks using 1/4" seam allowance.

3. Remove the paper from the quilt, leaving the paper on the outside edges until the last. Be careful when removing this paper as not to stretch the outside edges.

4. Quilt as desired.

5. Trim off excess batting and backing.

6. Sew on bias binding.

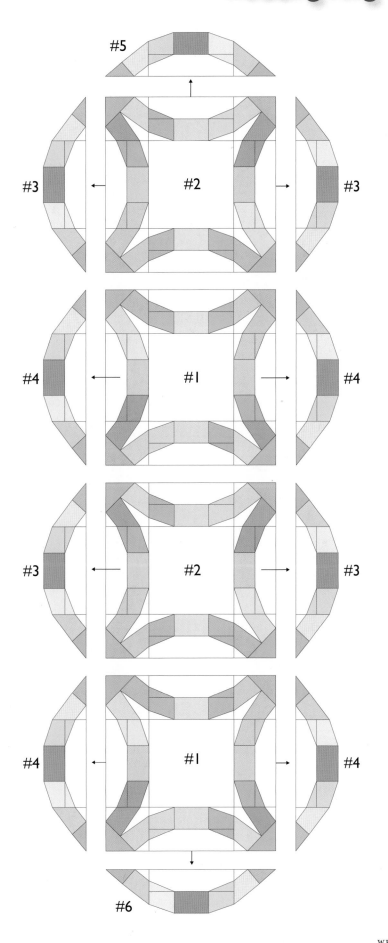

#5

#3   #2   #3

#4   #1   #4

#3   #2   #3

#4   #1   #4

#6

"Miniature Wedding Ring" made and quilted
by Carolyn Cullinan McCormick

Miniature Wedding Ring

14" x 14" Quilted • 9 - 4" Blocks • 12 – Outside Curved Blocks

CUTTING INSTRUCTIONS

From the background fabric, cut:

* Paper

✳ 1 – 3" x 27" strip. Cut the strip into 9 – 3" x 3" squares.

** No Paper

✳ 1 – 2 1/2" x 22 1/2" strip. Cut the strip into 9 – 2 1/2" squares.

✳ 2 – 3" strips. Cut the strips into 48 – 1 1/4" x 3" rectangles.

✳ 1 – 1 3/4" strip. Cut the strips into 36 – 1" x 1 3/4" rectangles.

✳ 2 – 1 1/2" strips. Cut the strips into 72 – 1" x 1 1/2" rectangles.

✳ 3 – 1 1/4" strips. Cut the strips into 96 – 1" x 1 1/4" rectangles.

From each of the 12 fat-eighth print fabrics, cut:

✳ 4 – 1 1/2" squares. You will have a total of 48 pieces.

✳ 10 – 1 1/4" x 1 1/2" rectangles. You will have a total of 120 pieces. Some of these pieces must match with units B & G. (See sewing units together.)

✳ 8 – 1" x 1 1/2" rectangles. You will have a total of 96 pieces. Some of these pieces must match with units A & F. (See sewing units together.)

✳ 6 – 1 1/4" x 1 3/4" rectangles. You will have a total of 72 pieces.

From the brown fabric, cut:

✳ 1 – 1 3/4" x 15 3/4" strip. Cut the strip into 9 – 1 3/4" x 1 3/4" squares. Cut the squares into half-square triangles.

✳ 1 – 1 1/2" x 15" strip. Cut the strip into 12 – 1 1/4" x 1 1/2" rectangles.

SUPPLY LIST

Units A & B – Make 36 Copies
Units C & D – Make 18 Copies
Unit E – Make 9 Copies (If using Paper)
Units F & G – Make 12 Copies
Units H & I – Make 6 Copies
Units J & K – Make 6 Copies

FABRICS:

Blocks	
Background	5/8 yd.
Print	12 Fat Eighths
Blue	Fat Eighth
Brown	Fat Eighth
Bias Binding	
Blue	Fat Quarter
Backing: 18" x 18"	
Batting: 18" x 18"	

From the blue fabric, cut:

✳ 1 – 1 3/4" x 15 3/4" strip. Cut the strips into 9 – 1 3/4" squares. Cut the squares into half-square triangles.

✳ 1 – 1 1/2" x 15" strip. Cut the strips into 12 – 1 1/4" x 1 1/2" rectangles.

BINDING:

From the blue fabric, cut:

✳ 66" of 2 1/4" bias binding.

---

* Paper – if using the paper template use this measurement.

** No Paper – if not placing the fabric on the paper template that is provided use this measurement.

PATTERN ON PAGE 119.

Miniature Wedding Ring

POSITION CHART: 9 - 4" BLOCKS

	Fabric	Position	Size
Unit A – Make 36	Print	1	1 1/2" x 1 1/2"
	***Print	2,3	1 1/4" x 1 1/2"
	Background	4,5	1" x 1 1/2"
Unit B –Make 36	Background	1	1 1/4" x 3"
	***Print	2,3	1" x 1 1/2"
Unit C – Make 18	Background	1	1" x 1 3/4"
	Print	2,3	1 1/4" x 1 3/4"
	Background	4,5	1" x 1 1/4"
	Brown	6	1 3/4" x 1 3/4"
Unit D - Make 18	Background	1	1" x 1 3/4"
	Print	2,3	1 1/4" x 1 3/4"
	Background	4,5	1" x 1 1/4"
	Blue	6	1 3/4" x 1 3/4"
Unit E –Make 9			
** No Paper	Background	1	2 1/2" x 2 1/2"
* Paper			3" x 3"

***It is very important to remember when sewing the fabrics onto units B2 and B3 that they must correspond with the fabrics on units A2 and A3.

SEWING DIRECTIONS: 9 - 4" BLOCKS

1. Follow the position chart and sew all fabric onto units A, B, C and D. If using paper for the center pieces (unit E), assemble as well.

2. It is very important to remember when sewing the fabrics onto units B2 and B3 that they must correspond with the fabrics on units A2 and A3.

3. Trim the units leaving 1/4" seam allowance.

4. Sew the units together following the diagram on how to assemble the block. Remove only the paper from the backside of the seam allowance; leave the remaining paper on until sewing the block to another block.

Sew units A to units B

Make 5 #1 blocks. **Note:** #1 and #2 blocks are all made using the same units. The only difference is the way they are pressed. Each block is pressed differently to make it easier for you to join the blocks together.

Sew units C and D to each side of units AB. Make 10 following these pressing arrows.

Sew units AB to each side of units E

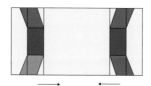

Sew together as shown

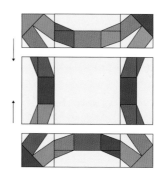

Make 4 – #2 blocks
Sew units C and D to each side of units AB
Make 8 following these pressing arrows.

Sew units AB to each side of units E

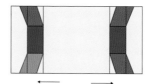

Sew together as shown

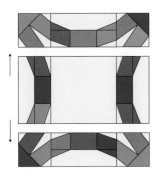

SEWING DIRECTIONS: OUTSIDE CURVED PIECES

1. Follow the position chart and sew all fabric onto units F, G, H, I, J and K.

2. It is very important to remember when sewing the fabrics onto units G2 and G3 that they must correspond with the fabrics on units F2 and F3.

3. Trim the units leaving 1/4" seam allowance.

4. Sew the units together following the diagram on how to assemble the curved block. Remove only the paper from the backside of the seam allowance; leave the remaining paper on until sewing the block to another block.

Make 12 - FGHI Outside Curves

Sew units F to units G

Sew units H and I to units FG
Make 4 - #3 blocks pressing as following.

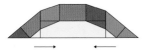

Make 2 - #4 blocks pressing as following.

POSITION CHART: OUTSIDE CURVES, 12 CURVES

	Fabric	Position	Size
Unit F – Make 12	Print	1	1 1/2" x 1 1/2"
	***Print	2,3	1 1/4" x 1 1/2"
Unit G –Make 12	Background	1	1 1/4" x 3"
	***Print	2,3	1" x 1 1/2"
Unit H – Make 6	Print	1	1 1/4" x 1 1/2"
	Background	2	1" x 1 1/4"
	Blue	3	1 1/4" x 1 1/2"
Unit I – Make 6	Print	1	1 1/4" x 1 1/2"
	Background	2	1" x 1 1/4"
	Brown	3	1 1/4" x 1 1/2"
Unit J –Make 6	Print	1	1 1/4" x 1 1/2"
	Background	2	1" x 1 1/4"
	Blue	3	1 1/4" x 1 1/2"
Unit K – Make 6	Print	1	1 1/4" x 1 1/2"
	Background	2	1" x 1 1/4"
	Brown	3	1 1/4" x 1 1/2"

***It is very important to remember when sewing the fabrics onto units G2 and G3 that they must correspond with the fabrics on units F2 and F3.

Sew units J and K to units FD
Make 4 - #5 blocks pressing as following.

Make 2 - #6 blocks pressing as following.

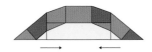

Miniature Wedding Ring

ASSEMBLING THE QUILT

1. Before assembling the quilt it is very important to sew (stay stitch) 1/8" on the curve of the outside pieces. This will help to stabilize the fabric when removing the paper.

2. Refer to the diagram and sew the outside curves to the blocks using 1/4" seam allowance. Sew the blocks together in rows.

3. Remove the paper from the quilt, leaving the paper on the outside edges until the last. Be careful when removing this paper as not to stretch the outside edges.

4. Quilt as desired.

5. Trim off excess batting and backing.

6. Sew on bias binding.

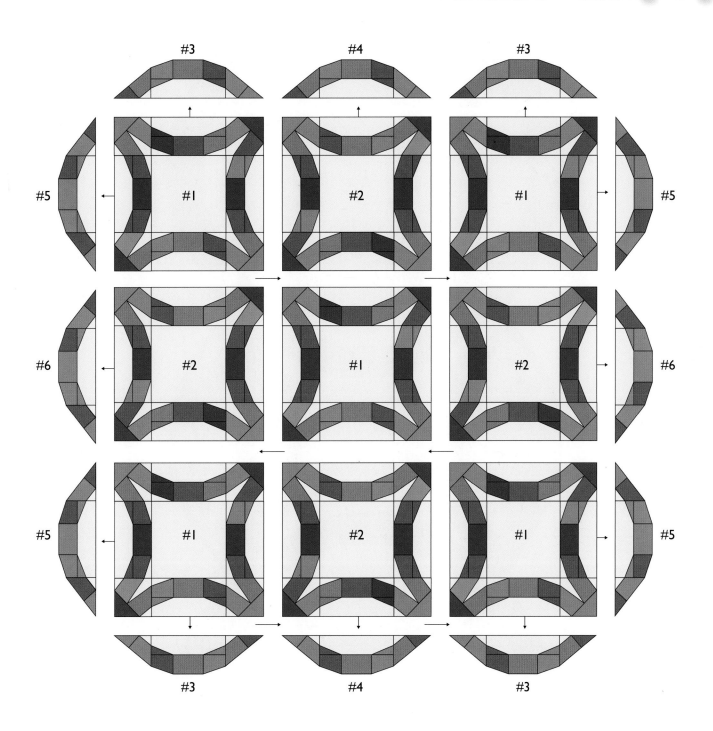

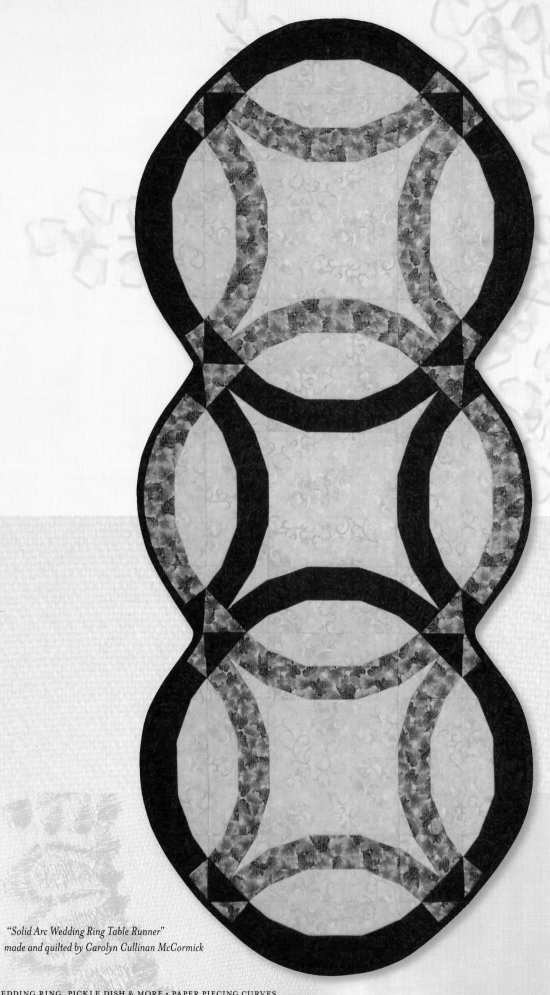

"Solid Arc Wedding Ring Table Runner"
made and quilted by Carolyn Cullinan McCormick

Solid Arc Wedding Ring Table Runner

Variation of Wedding Ring October 1928 • 18 1/2" x 41 1/2" Quilted
3 – 12" Blocks • 2 – Medium Outside Edge • 6 – Dark Outside Edge

CUTTING INSTRUCTIONS

From the background fabric, cut:

✱ 2 – 7" strips. Cut the strips into 20 – 2 1/2" x 7" rectangles.

* Paper

✱ 1 – 7" x 21" strip. Cut the strip into 3 – 7" squares.

** No Paper

✱ 1 – 6 1/2" x 19 1/2" strip. Cut the strip into 3 – 6 1/2" squares.

✱ 1 – 3 3/4" x 24" strip. Cut the strip into 12 – 2" x 3 3/4" rectangles.

✱ 1 – 3" x 42" strip. Cut the strip into 24 – 1 1/2" x 3" rectangles.

✱ 2 – 2 1/4" strips. Cut the strips into 40 – 1 1/2" x 2 1/4" rectangles.

From the medium fabric, cut:

✱ 1 – 7" x 22 1/2" strip. Cut the strip into 10 – 2 1/4" x 7" rectangles.

✱ 1 – 3 1/2" x 36" strip and 1 – 3 1/2" x 7" strip. Cut the strips into 16 – 2 1/4" x 3 1/2" rectangles and 2 – 3 1/2" squares. Cut the squares into 4 half-square triangles.

✱ 1 – 3 1/4" x 10" strip. Cut the strip into 4 – 2 1/2" x 3 1/4" rectangles.

✱ 1 – 3" x 30" strip. Cut the strip 20 – 1 1/2" x 3" rectangles.

✱ 1 – 2 1/2" x 27" strip. Cut the strip into 12 – 2 1/4" x 2 1/2" rectangles.

From the dark fabric, cut:

✱ 1 – 7" x 22 1/2" strip. Cut the strip into 10 – 2 1/4" x 7" rectangles.

✱ 1 – 3 1/2" x 32" strip. Cut the strip into 8 – 2 1/4" x 3 1/2" rectangles and 4 – 3 1/2" squares. Cut the squares into 8 half-square triangles.

✱ 1 – 3 1/4" x 30" strip. Cut the strip into 12 – 2 1/2" x 3 1/4" rectangles.

✱ 1 – 3" x 30" strip. Cut the strip into 20 – 1 1/2" x 3" rectangles.

✱ 1 – 2 1/2" x 9" strip. Cut the strip into 4 – 2 1/4" x 2 1/2" rectangles.

BINDING:

From the dark fabric, cut:

✱ 125" - 2 1/2" bias binding.

SUPPLY LIST

Unit A – Make 12 Copies
Unit B – Make 12 Copies
Unit C – Make 3 Copies (If using Paper)
Unit D – Make 8 Copies
Unit E & F– Make 2 Copies Each
Unit G & H– Make 6 Copies Each

FABRICS:

Blocks		
Background	1 yd.	
Medium	3/4 yd.	
Dark	3/4 yd.	
Binding		
Dark	1/2 yd.	

Batting: 22" x 45"
Backing: 22" x 45"

---

* Paper – if using the paper template use this measurement.

** No Paper – if not placing the fabric on the paper template that is provided use this measurement.

PATTERN ON PAGES 120 – 122.

Solid Arc Wedding Ring Table Runner

POSITION CHART: 3 -12" BLOCKS

	Fabric	Position	Size
Unit A – Make	Background	1	2 1/2" x 7"
8 Medium	Medium	2,3	1 1/2" x 3"
	Medium	4	2 1/4" x 7"
	Background	5,6	1 1/2" x 3"
Unit A – Make	Background	1	2 1/2" x 7"
4 Dark	Dark	2,3	1 1/2" x 3"
	Dark	4	2 1/4" x 7"
	Background	5,6	1 1/2" x 3"
Unit B – Make	Background	1	2" x 3 3/4"
8 Medium	Medium	2,3	2 1/4" x 3 1/2"
	Background	4,5	1 1/2" x 2 1/4"
	Dark	6	3 1/2" x 3 1/2" ◣
Unit B – Make	Background	1	2" x 3 3/4"
4 Dark	Dark	2,3	2 1/4" x 3 1/2"
	Background	4,5	1 1/2" x 2 1/4"
	Medium	6	3 1/2" x 3 1/2" ◣
Unit C – Make 3			
** No Paper	Background	1	6 1/2" x 6 1/2"
*Paper			7" x 7"

SEWING DIRECTIONS: BLOCKS

1. Follow the position chart and sew all fabric onto units A and B. Make 2 blocks with the medium fabric and 1 block with the dark fabric. If using paper for the center pieces (unit C), assemble as well.

2. Trim the units leaving a 1/4" seam allowance.

3. Sew the units together following the diagram on how to assemble the block. Remove only the paper from the backside of the seam allowance; leave the remaining paper on until sewing the block to another block.

Make 2 Medium Blocks

Sew units A to units B. Make 4

Sew units C to units AB. Make 2.

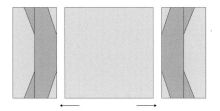

Sew together as shown.

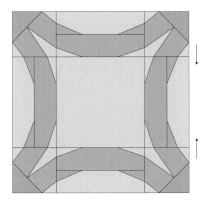

Make 1 Dark Block

Sew units A to units B. Make 2

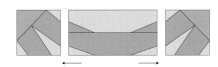

Sew units C to units AB. Make 1

Sew together as shown

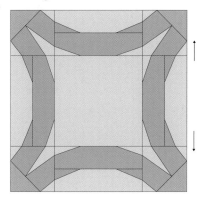

SEWING DIRECTIONS: OUTSIDE CURVED PIECES

1. Follow the position chart and sew all fabric onto units D, E and F. Make 9 outside curves with medium fabric and 9 outside curves with the dark fabric.

2. Trim the units leaving 1/4" seam allowance.

3. Sew the units together following the diagram on how to assemble the curved block. Remove only the paper from the backside of the seam allowance; leave the remaining paper on until sewing the block to another block.

Make 2 Medium Curves

Sew units E and F to units D.

Make 6 Dark Curves

Sew units G and H to units D

POSITION CHART: OUTSIDE EDGE, 2 – MEDIUM, 6 – DARK			
	Fabric	Position	Size
Unit D – Make	Background	1	2 1/2" x 7"
2 Medium	Medium	2,3	1 1/2" x 3"
	Medium	4	2 1/4" x 7"
Unit D – Make	Background	1	2 1/2" x 7"
6 Dark	Dark	2,3	1 1/2" x 3"
	Dark	4	2 1/4" x 7"
Units E & F – Make	Medium	1	2 1/2" x 3 1/4"
2 each Medium	Background	2	1 1/2" x 2 1/4"
	Dark	3	2 1/4" x 2 1/2"
Units G & H –	Dark	1	2 1/2" x 3 1/4"
Make 6 each	Background	2	1 1/2" x 2 1/4"
Dark	Medium	3	2 1/4" x 2 1/2"

Solid Arc Wedding Ring Table Runner

ASSEMBLING THE QUILT

1. Before assembling the quilt, sew (stay stitch) 1/8" on the curve of the outside pieces. This will help to stabilize the fabric when removing the paper.

2. Refer to the diagram and sew the outside curves to the blocks using 1/4" seam allowance.

3. Remove the paper from the quilt, leaving the paper on the outside edges until the last. Be careful when removing this paper as not to stretch the outside edges.

4. Quilt as desired.

5. Trim off excess batting and backing.

6. Sew on bias binding.

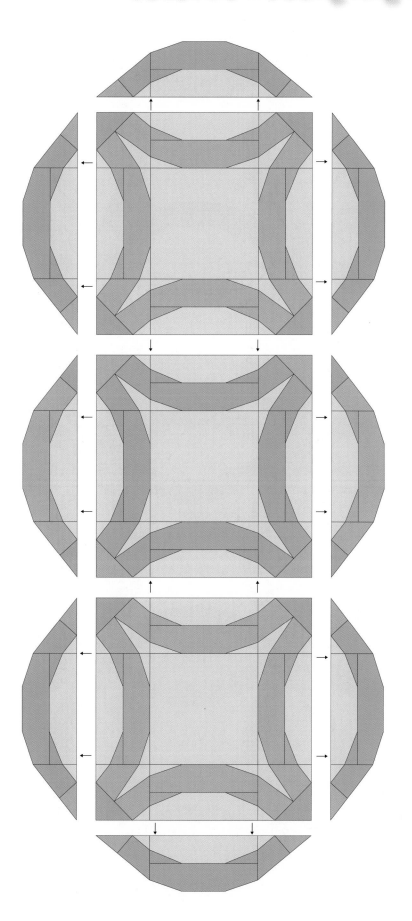

Miniature Solid Arc Wedding Ring

Variation of Wedding Ring October 1928 • 14" x 18" Quilted

12 – 4" Blocks • 7 – Medium Outside Edges • 7 – Dark Outside Edges

CUTTING INSTRUCTIONS

From the background fabric, cut:

✱ 2 – 3" strips. Cut the strips into 62 – 1 1/4" x 3" rectangles.

* Paper

✱ 1 – 3" strip. Cut the strip into 12 – 3" squares.

** No Paper

✱ 1 – 2 1/2" strip. Cut the strip into 12 – 2 1/2" squares.

✱ 2 – 1 3/4" strips. Cut the strips into 48 – 1" x 1 3/4" rectangles.

✱ 6 – 1 1/4" strips. Cut the strips into 220 – 1" x 1 1/4" rectangles.

From the medium fabric, cut:

✱ 1 – 3" strips. Cut the strips into 31 – 1 1/4" x 3" rectangles.

✱ 1 – 1 3/4" strip. Cut the strip into 12 – 1 3/4" squares. Cut the squares into 24 half-square triangles.

✱ 3 – 1 1/2" strips. Cut the strips into 48 – 1 1/2" squares.

✱ 2 – 1 1/4" strips. Cut the strips into 62– 3/4" x 1 1/4" rectangles

From the dark fabric, cut:

✱ 1 – 3" strips. Cut the strips into 31 – 1 1/4" x 3" rectangles.

✱ 1 – 1 3/4" strip. Cut the strip into 12 – 1 3/4" squares. Cut the squares into 24 half-square triangles.

✱ 3 – 1 1/2" strips. Cut the strips into 48 –1 1/2" squares and 28 – 1 1/4" x 1 1/2" rectangles.

✱ 2 – 1 1/4" strips. Cut the strips into 62 – 3/4" x 1 1/4" rectangles.

SUPPLY LIST

Unit A – Make 48 Copies
Unit B – Make 48 Copies
Unit C – Make 12 Copies (If using Paper)
Unit D – Make 14 Copies
Unit E & F– Make 7 Copies Each
Unit G & H– Make 7 Copies Each

FABRICS:

Blocks

Background	3/4 yd.	
Medium	3/8 yd.	
Dark	3/8 yd.	

Binding

Dark	1 fat quarter

Batting: 18" x 22"

Backing: 1 fat quarter

BINDING:

From the black fabric, cut:

✱ 80" – 2 1/4" bias binding.

> * Paper – if using the paper template use this measurement.
>
> ** No Paper – if not placing the fabric on the paper template that is provided use this measurement.

PATTERN ON PAGE 123.

Opposite: "Miniature Solid Arc Wedding Ring" made and quilted by Carolyn Cullinan McCormick

Miniature Solid Arc Wedding Ring

POSITION CHART: 12 - 4" BLOCKS

	Fabric	Position	Size
Unit A – Make	Background	1	1 1/4" x 3"
24 Dark	Dark	2,3	3/4" x 1 1/4"
	Dark	4	1 1/4" x 3"
	Background	5,6	1" x 1 1/4"
Unit A – Make	Background	1	1 1/4" x 3"
24 Medium	Medium	2,3	3/4" x 1 1/4"
	Medium	4	1 1/4" x 3"
	Background	5,6	1" x 1 1/4"
Unit B – Make	Background	1	1" x 1 3/4"
24 Dark	Dark	2,3	1 1/2" x 1 1/2"
	Background	4,5	1" x 1 1/4"
	Medium	6	1 3/4" x 1 3/4"
Unit B – Make	Background	1	1" x 1 3/4"
24 Medium	Medium	2,3	1 1/2" x 1 1/2"
	Background	4,5	1" x 1 1/4"
	Dark	6	1 3/4" x 1 3/4"
Unit C – Make 12			
** No Paper	Background	1	2 1/2" x 2 1/2"
*Paper			3" x 3"

SEWING DIRECTIONS: 12 – 4" BLOCKS

1. Follow the position chart and sew all fabric onto units A and B. Make 6 blocks with the medium fabric and 6 blocks with the dark fabric. If using paper for the center pieces (unit C), assemble as well.

2. Trim the units leaving a 1/4" seam allowance.

3. Sew the units together following the diagram on how to assemble the block. Remove only the paper from the backside of the seam allowance; leave the remaining paper on until sewing the block to another block.

   Make 6 Medium Blocks
   Sew units A to units B. Make 12

Sew units C to units AB. Make 6.

Sew together as shown.

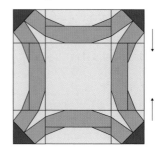

Make 6 Dark Blocks

Sew units A to units B. Make 12

Sew units C to units AB. Make 6

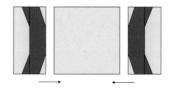

Sew together as shown

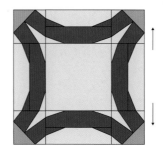

SEWING DIRECTIONS: OUTSIDE CURVED PIECES

1. Follow the position chart and sew all fabric onto units D, E and F. Make 7 outside curves with medium fabric and 7 outside curves with the dark fabric.

2. Trim the units leaving 1/4" seam allowance.

3. Sew the units together following the diagram on how to assemble the curved block. Remove only the paper from the backside of the seam allowance; leave the remaining paper on until sewing the block to another block.

Make 7 Medium Curves

Sew units E and F to units D.

Make 7 Dark Curves

Sew units G and H to units D

POSITION CHART: 7 – DARK OUT-SIDE CURVES, 7 – MEDIUM OUT-SIDE CURVES

	Fabric	Position	Size
Unit D –	Background	1	1 1/4" x 3"
Make 7 Dark	Dark	2,3	3/4" x 1 1/4"
	Dark	4	1 1/4" x 3"
Unit D –	Background	1	1 1/4" x 3"
Make 7 Medium	Medium	2,3	3/4" x 1 1/4"
	Medium	4	1 1/4" x 3"
Units E & F	Medium	1	1 1/4" x 1 1/2"
– Make 7 each	Background	2	1" x 1 1/4"
	Dark	3	1 1/4" x 1 1/2"
Units G & H –	Dark	1	1 1/4" x 1 1/2"
Make 7 each	Background	2	1" x 1 1/4"
	Medium	3	1 1/4" x 1 1/2"

Miniature Solid Arc Wedding Ring

ASSEMBLING THE QUILT

1. Before assembling the quilt, sew (stay stitch) 1/8" on the curve of the outside pieces. This will help to stabilize the fabric when removing the paper.

2. Refer to the diagram and sew the outside curves to the blocks using 1/4" seam allowance. Sew the blocks together.

3. Remove the paper from the quilt, leaving the paper on the outside edges until the last. Be careful not to stretch the outside edges when removing the paper.

4. Quilt as desired.

5. Trim off excess batting and backing.

6. Sew on bias binding.

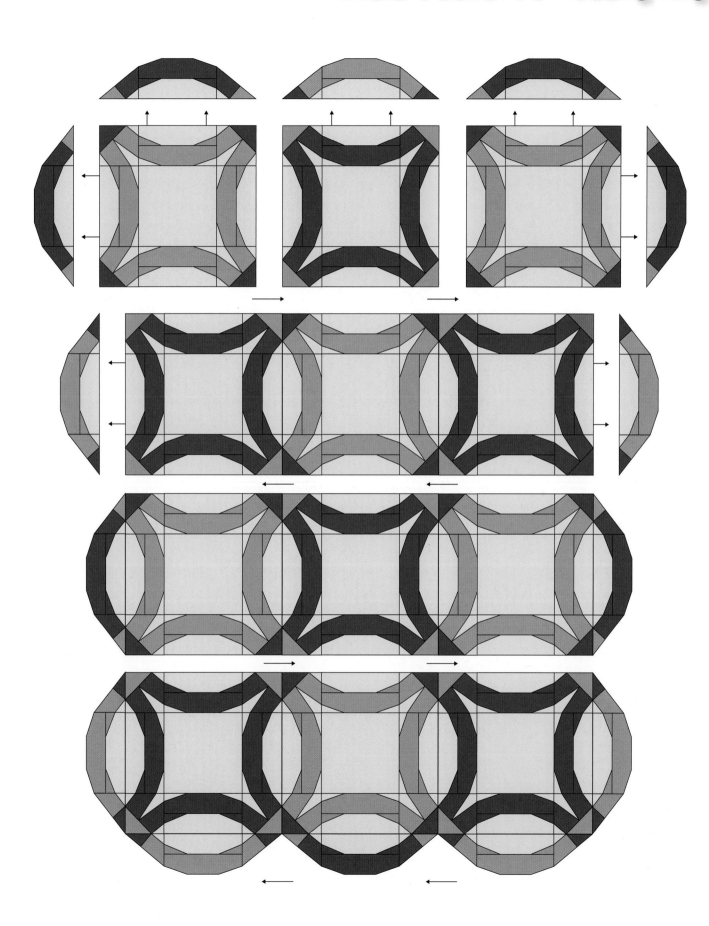

Gallery

Lovely variations on our themes

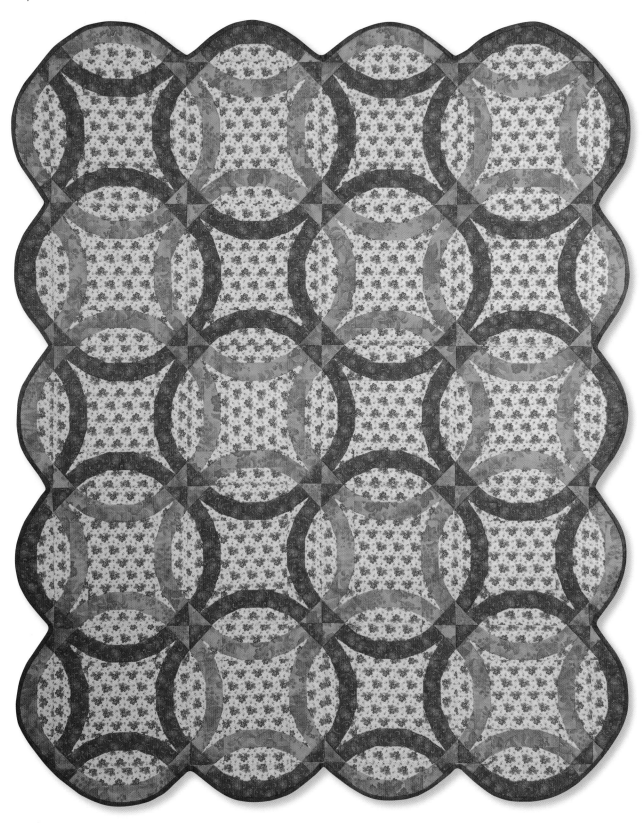

Opposite page: *"Solid Arc Wedding Ring" made by Brenda Phillips, Sedalia, Colorado, Polly Somers, Sedalia, Colorado and Jeannine Glendenning, Castle Rock, Colorado, quilted by Susan Bateman, Parker, Colorado.* **Above:** *"Pickle Dish" made by Carol Netwal, Castle Rock, Colorado, quilted by Carol Willey, Castle Rock, Colorado.* **Left:** *"Four Leaf Clover" made by Kelly Collins, Littleton, Colorado, and Pat Prestridge, San Antonio, Texas. Quilted by Kelly Collins.*

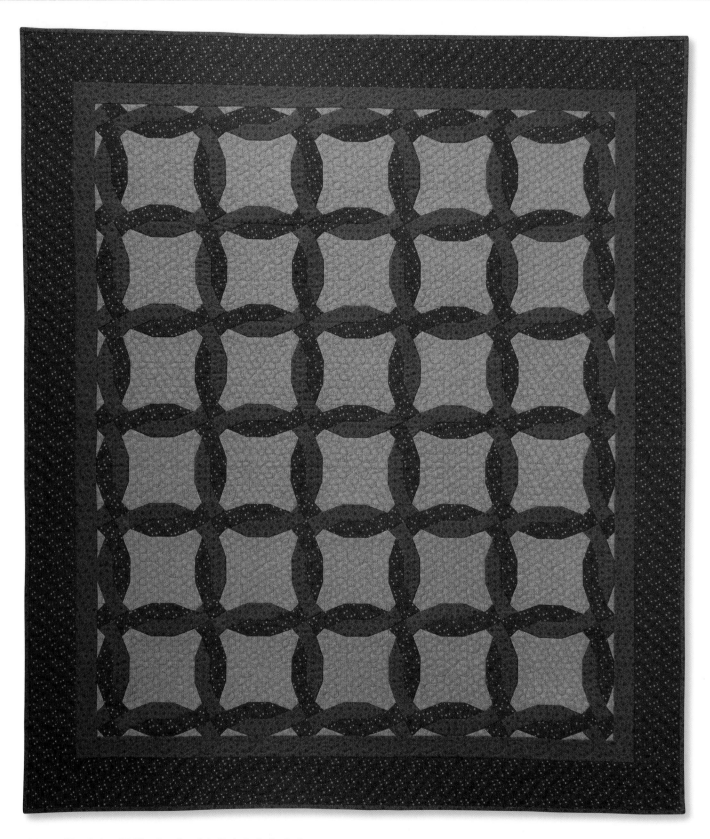

Above: *"Interlocking Wedding Rings" made by Kathy Rutkosky, Larkspur, Colorado and quilted by Jan Korytkowski, Castle Rock, Colorado.*
Right: *"Jake" made by Marie Huber, Glendive, Montana, quilted by Jan Holden, Glendive, Montana. Fabric by Marcus Brothers.*

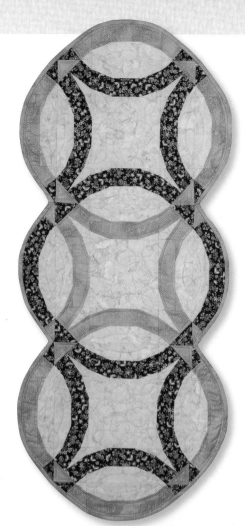

Above: *"Wedding Ring" stitched by Megan McCormick, Parker, Colorado, quilted by Carol Willey, Castle Rock, Colorado.*
Above right: *"Wedding Ring" wall hanging made by Karon Larson, La Crosse, Wisconsin, quilted by Betty Kane, La Crosse, Wisconsin.*
Right: *"Rob Peter and Pay Paul" made and quilted by Carol Bonetti, Castle Rock, Colorado.*

"Wedding Ring" made by Megan McCormick, Parker, Colorado, Carol Netwal, Castle Rock, Colorado, Sandy Reinke, Lakewood, Colorado, Meriellen Joga, Castle Rock, Kelly Collins, Littleton, Colorado and Connie Samora, Castle Rock, quilted by Carol Willey, Castle Rock, Colorado. Fabric by Marcus Brothers.

"Hands all 'Round" made and quilted by Marilyn Vap,
Castle Rock, Colorado.

"Hands all 'Round" made by Carolyn Cullinan McCormick,
quilted by Carol Willey, Castle Rock, Colorado. Fabric by Batik Textiles.

Above: *"The Broken Stone" made and quilted by Megan McCormick Parker, Colorado. Fabric by Timeless Treasures.*
Right: *"Lafayette Orange Peel" made and quilted by Julie Lilly, Monument, Colorado.*

"The Flower Ring" made and quilted by Meriellen Joga,
Castle Rock, Colorado.

Wedding Ring

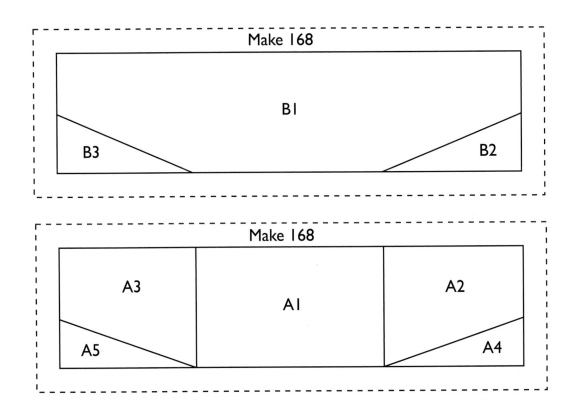

Wedding Ring

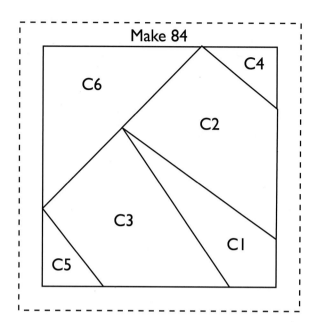

Make 84

C6 C4 C2 C3 C1 C5

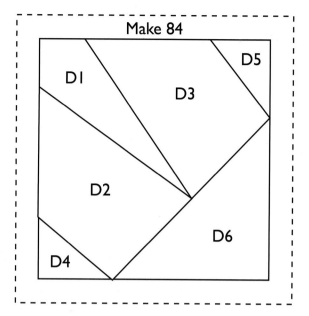

Make 84

D1 D3 D5 D2 D6 D4

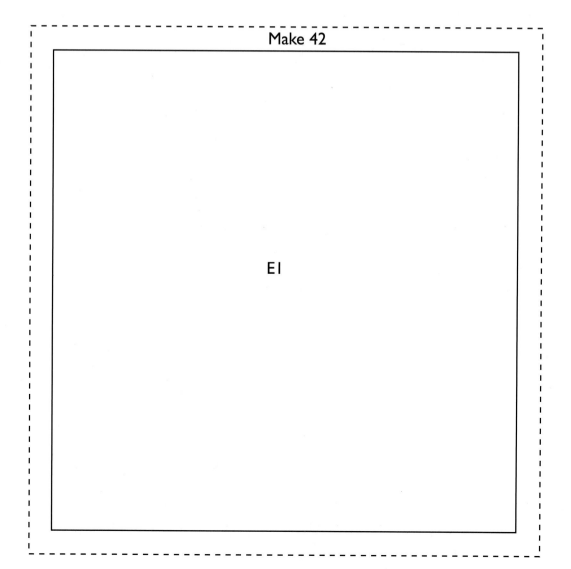

Make 42

E1

Wedding Ring

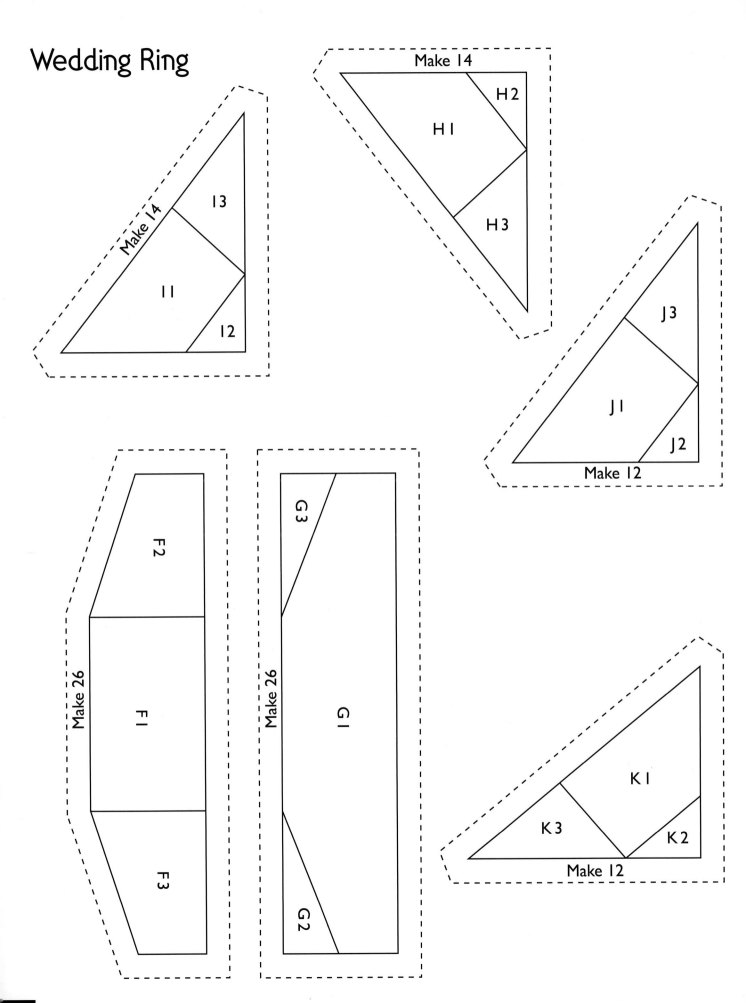

Make 14

H1 H2 H3

I3 I1 I2
Make 14

J3 J1 J2
Make 12

F2 F1 F3
Make 26

G3 G1 G2
Make 26

K1 K3 K2
Make 12

Pickle Dish

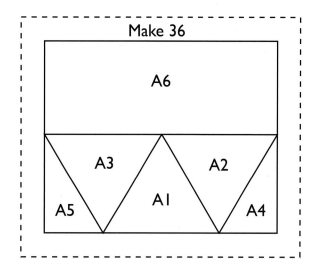

Make 36

A6
A3 A2
A5 A1 A4

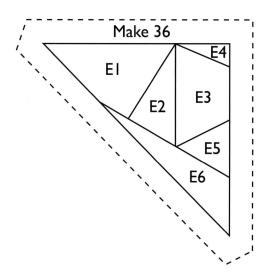

Make 36

E1 E4
E2 E3
E5
E6

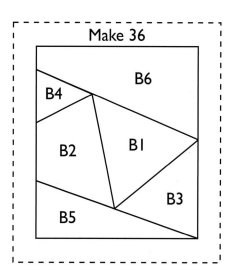

Make 36

B4 B6
B2 B1
B5 B3

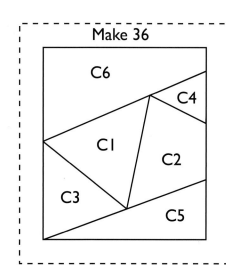

Make 36

C6
C4
C1 C2
C3 C5

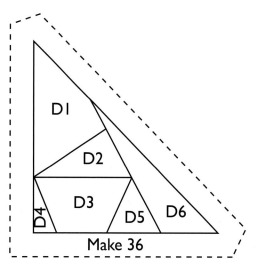

D1
D2
D3 D5 D6
D4

Make 36

Pickle Dish

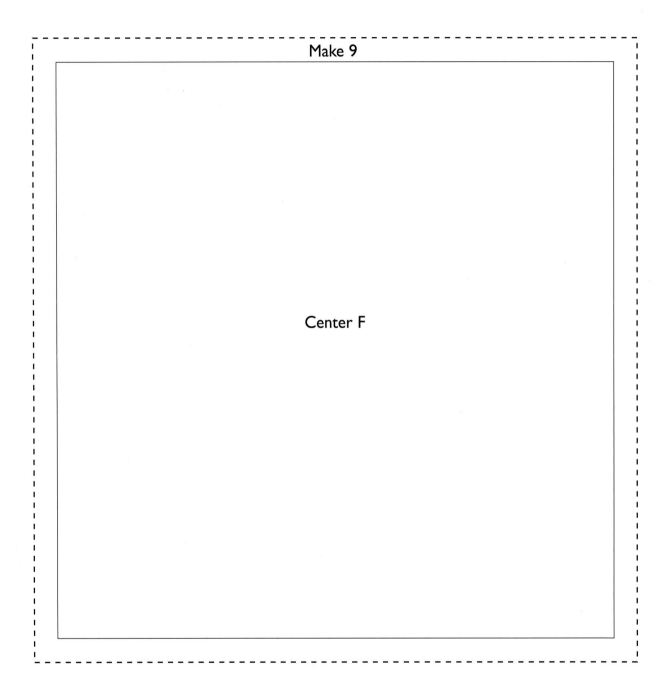

Make 9

Center F

Pickle Dish

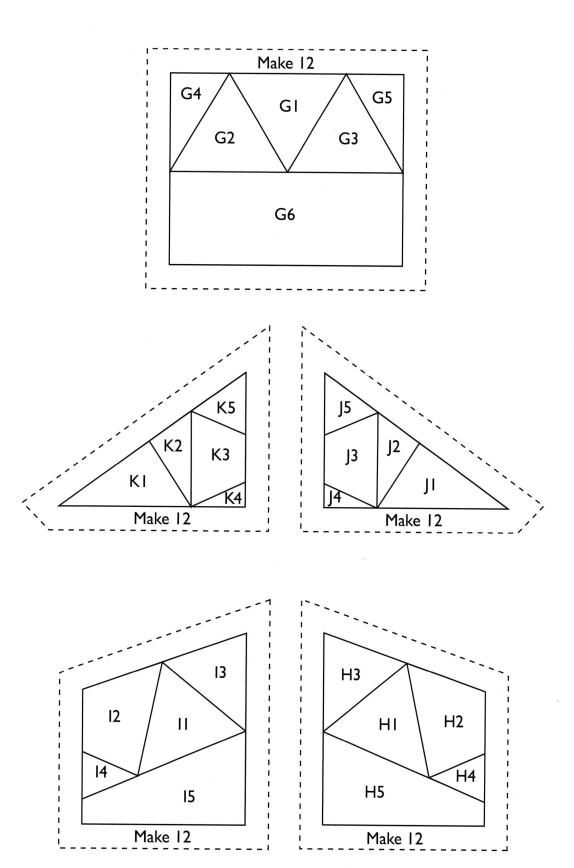

Solid Arc Wedding Ring

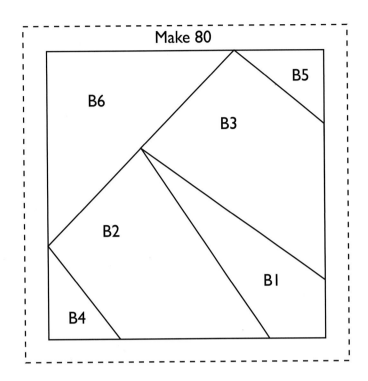

Make 80

B5
B6
B3
B2
B1
B4

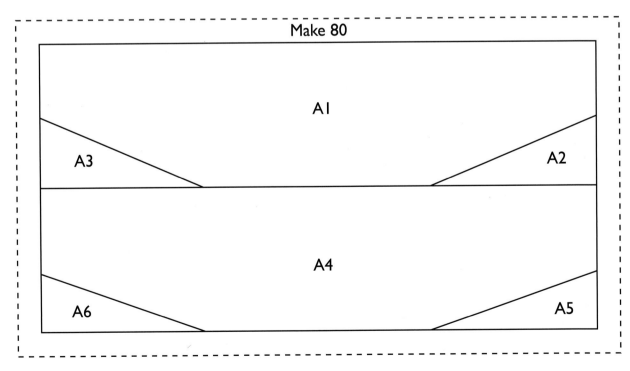

Make 80

A1
A3
A2
A4
A6
A5

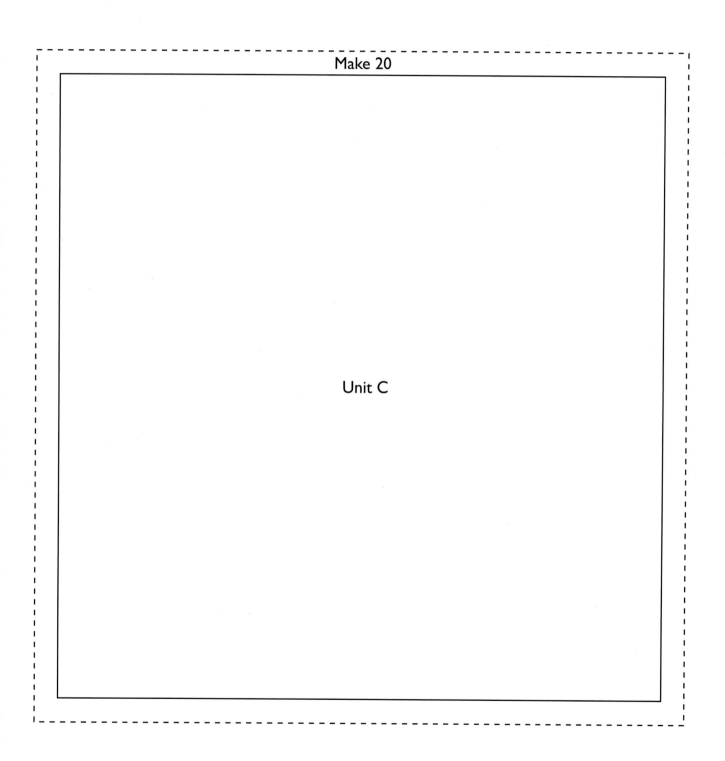

Make 20

Unit C

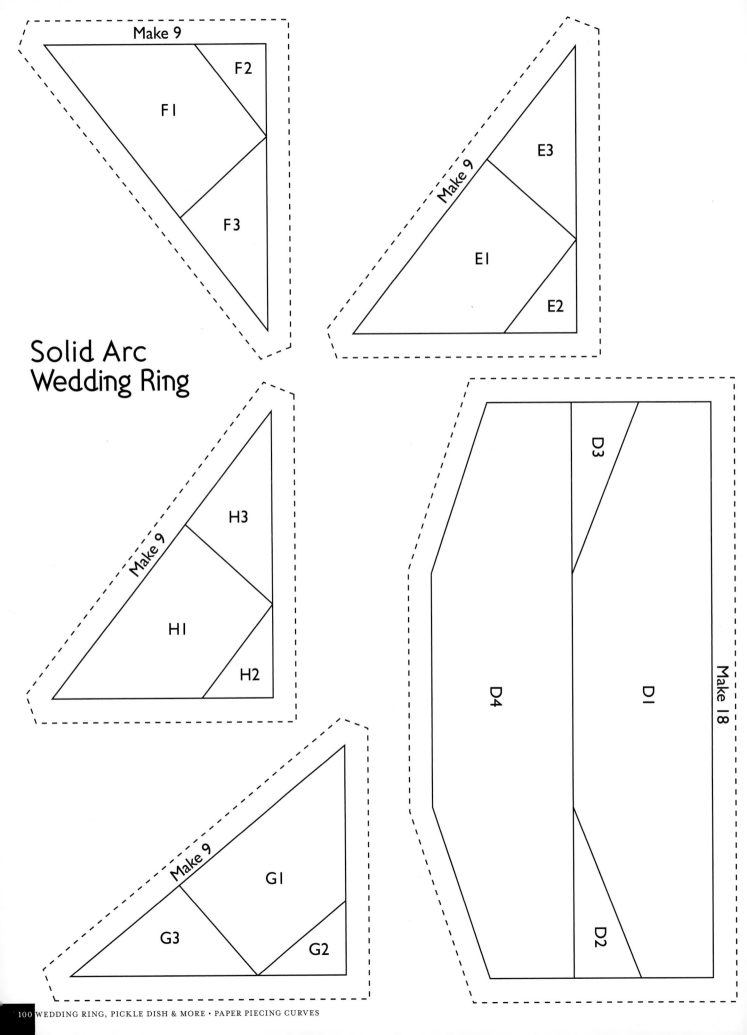

Solid Arc
Wedding Ring

Make 9

F2

F1

F3

Make 9

E3

E1

E2

Make 9

H3

H1

H2

Make 9

G1

G3

G2

D3

D4

D1

D2

Make 18

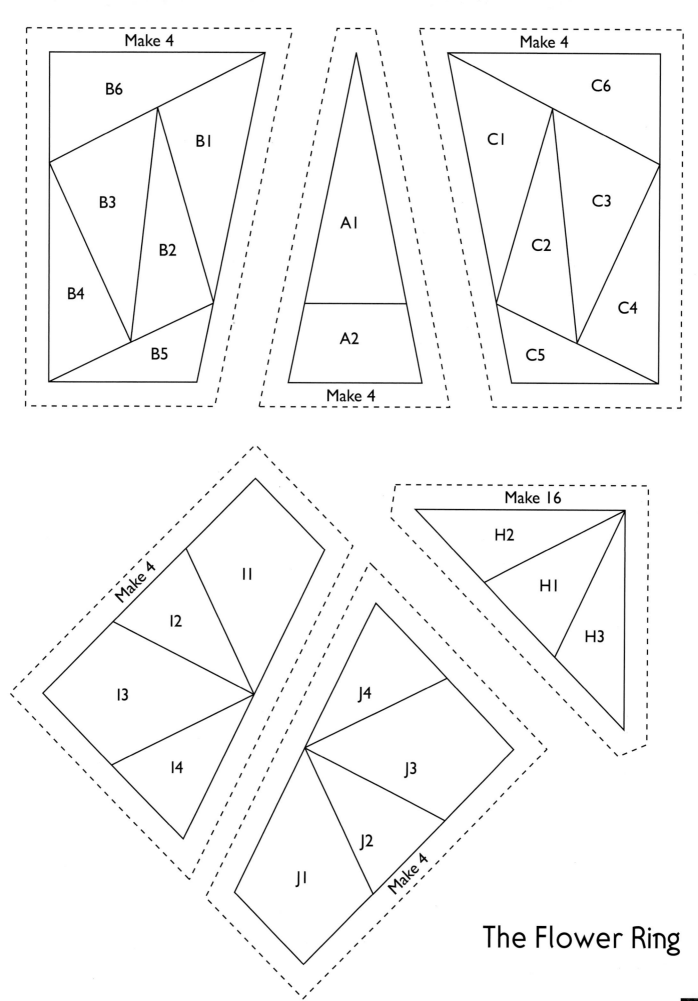

Make 4

B6

B1

B3

B2

B4

B5

A1

A2

Make 4

Make 4

C6

C1

C3

C2

C4

C5

Make 16

H2

H1

H3

Make 4

I1

I2

I3

I4

J4

J3

J2

J1

Make 4

The Flower Ring

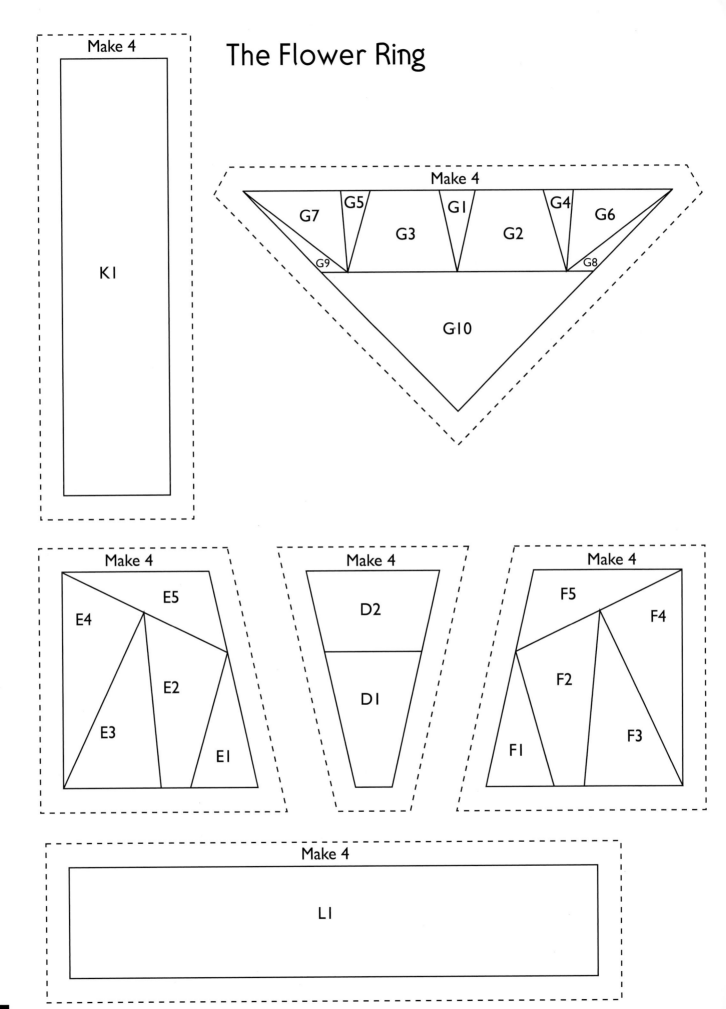

The Flower Ring

Make 4

K1

Make 4

G7 G5 G1 G4 G6
G3 G2
G9 G8
G10

Make 4

E4 E5
E2
E3 E1

Make 4

D2
D1

Make 4

F5 F4
F2
F1 F3

Make 4

L1

Rob Peter and Pay Paul

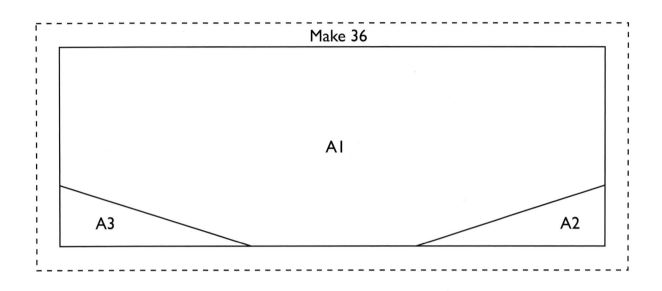

Make 36

A1

A3

A2

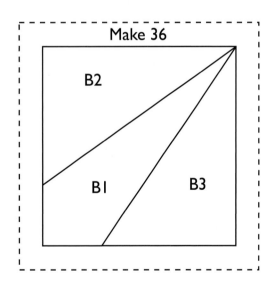

Make 36

B2

B1

B3

Rob Peter and Pay Paul

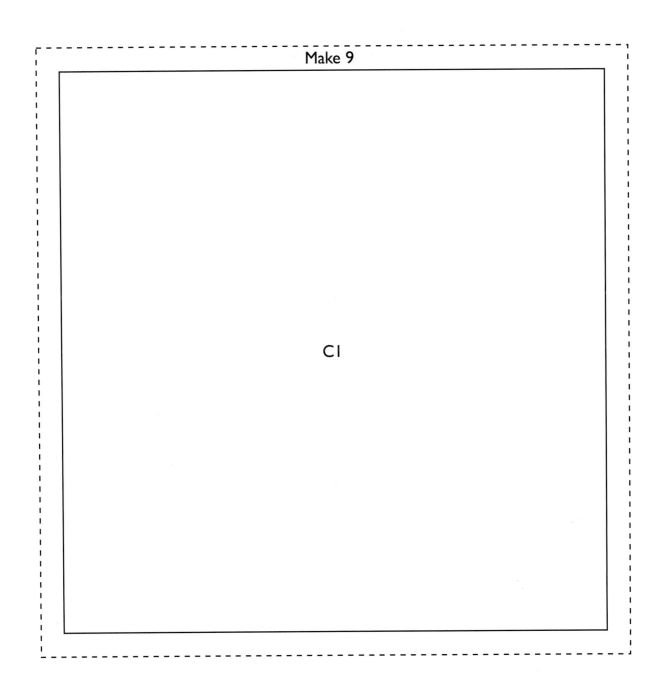

Make 9

CI

Rob Peter and Pay Paul

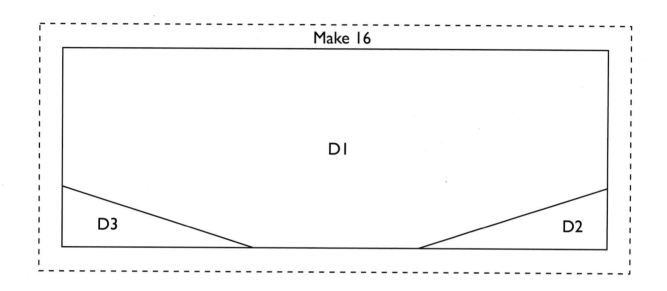

Make 16

D1

D3   D2

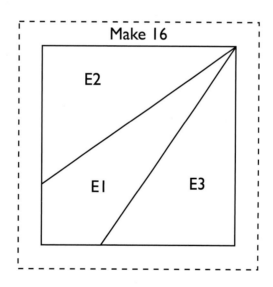

Make 16

E2

E1   E3

Rob Peter and Pay Paul

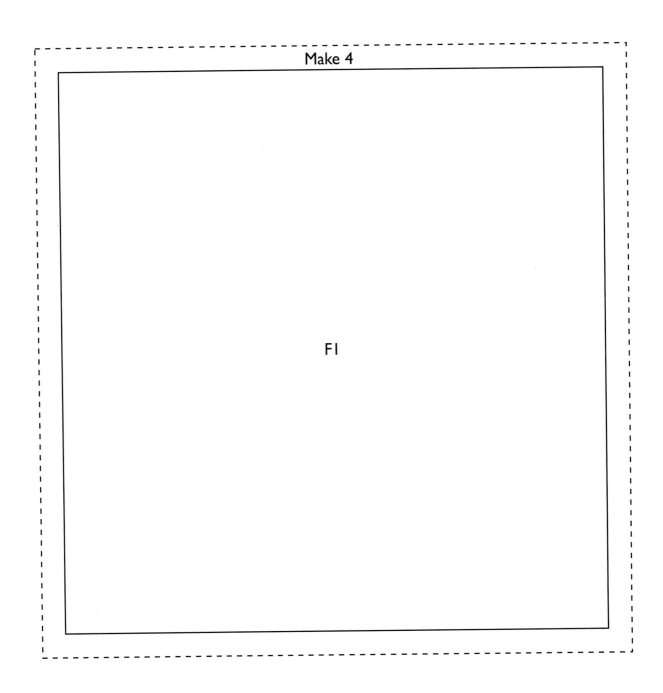

Make 4

F1

The Broken Stone

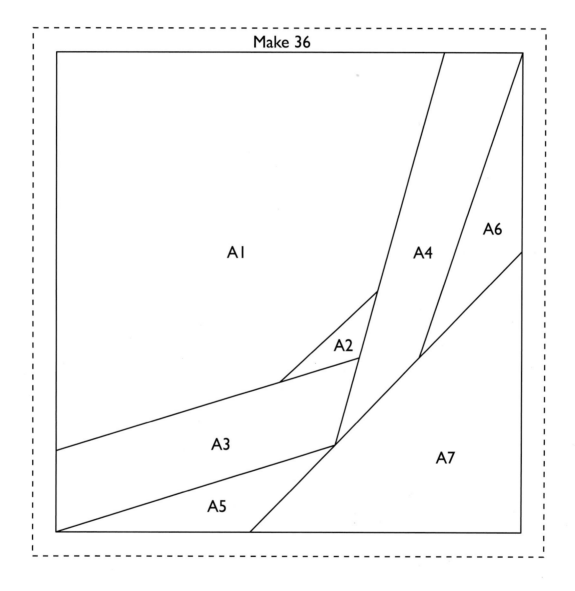

Make 36

A1
A2
A3
A4
A5
A6
A7

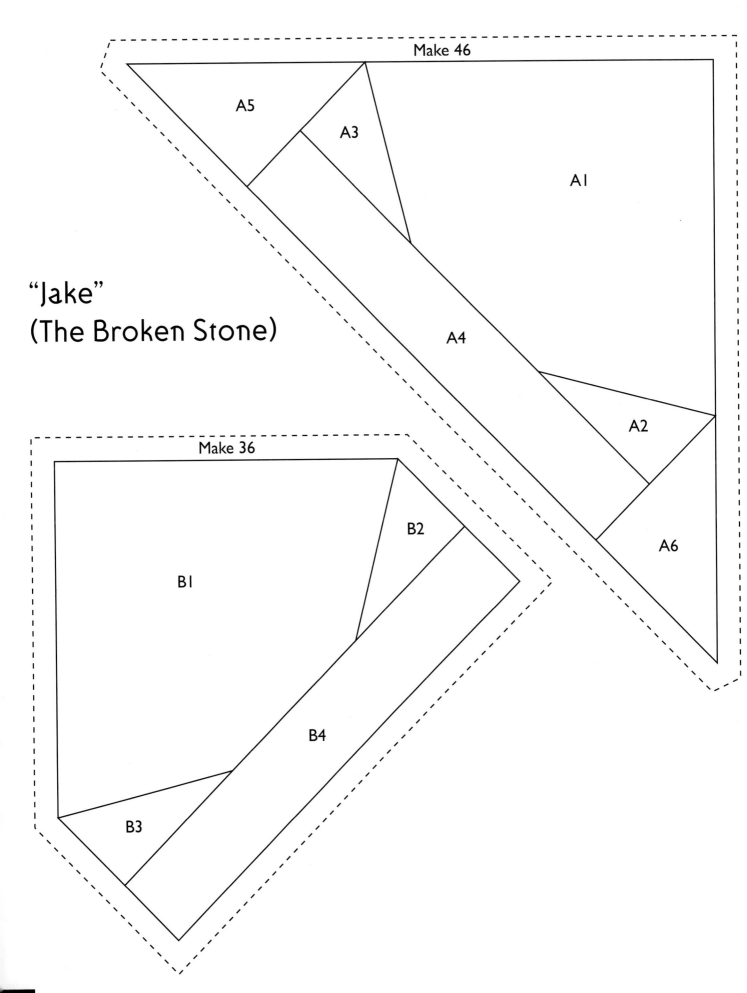

"Jake"
(The Broken Stone)

Make 46

A5

A3

A1

A4

A2

A6

Make 36

B2

B1

B4

B3

"Jake" (The Broken Stone)

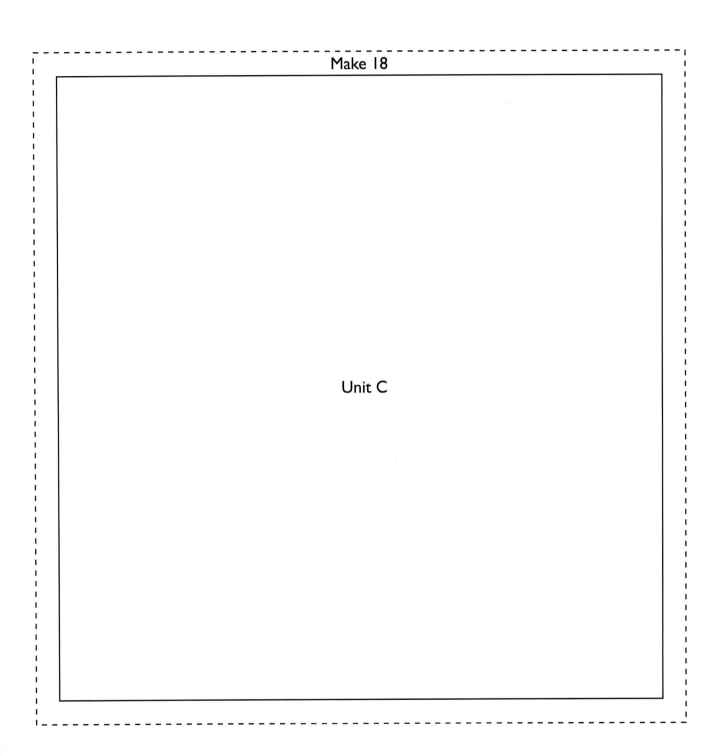

Make 18

Unit C

Hands all 'Round

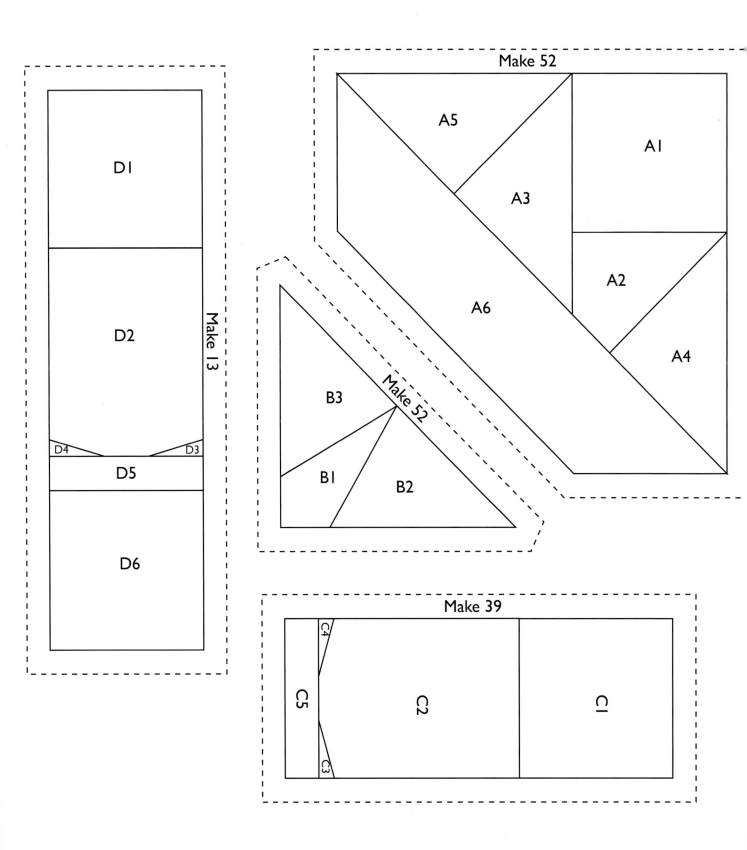

Make 52

A5

A1

A3

A6

A2

A4

D1

D2

Make 13

D4   D3

D5

D6

B3

Make 52

B1

B2

Make 39

C4

C5

C2

C1

C3

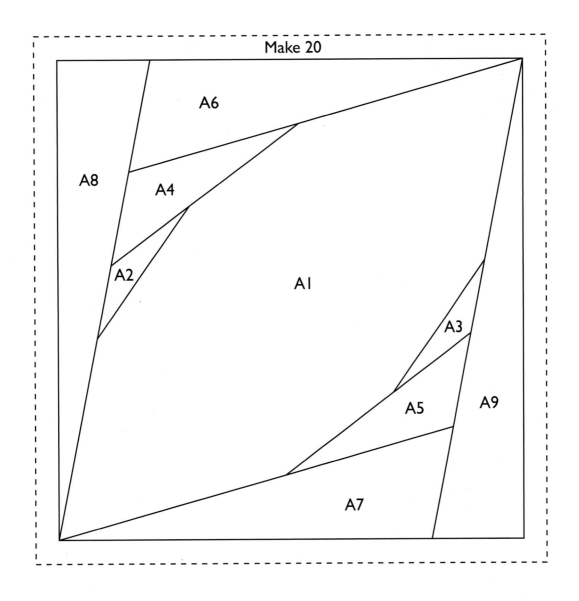

Make 20

A6

A8

A4

A2

A1

A3

A5

A9

A7

Interlocked Wedding Rings

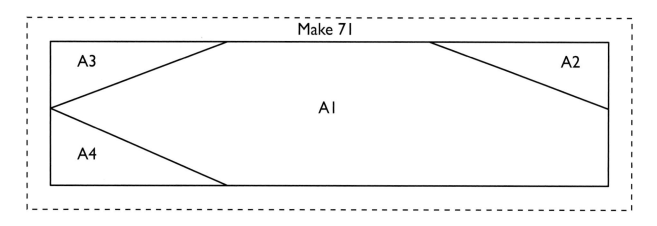

Make 71

A3 A2 A1 A4

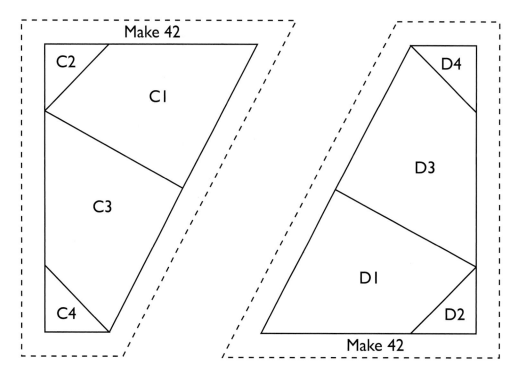

Make 42

C2 C1 C3 C4

D4 D3 D1 D2

Make 42

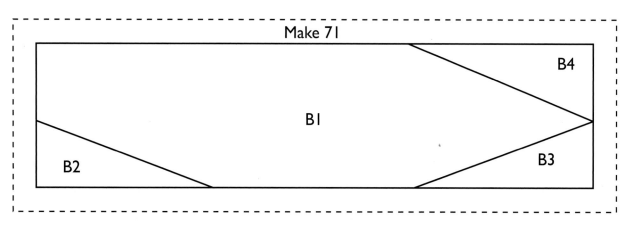

Make 71

B1 B2 B4 B3

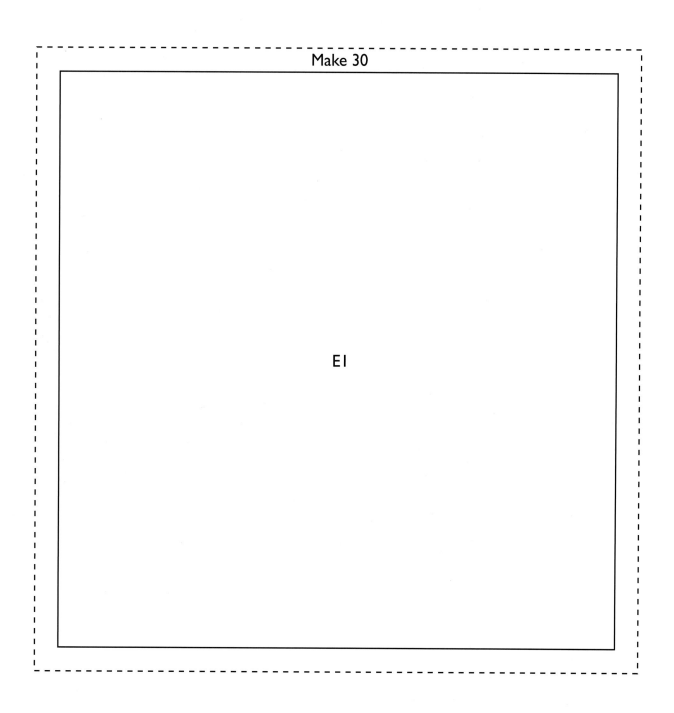

Make 30

E1

Four Leaf Clover

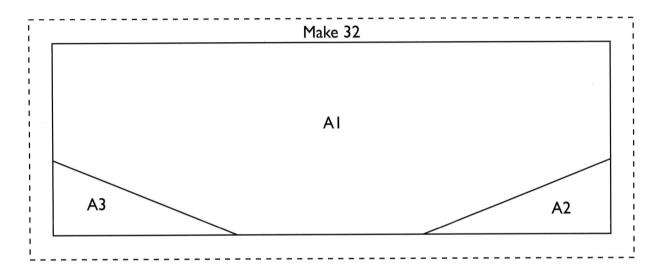

Make 32

A1

A3

A2

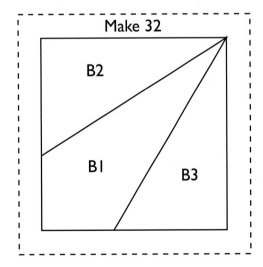

Make 32

B2

B1

B3

Four Leaf Clover

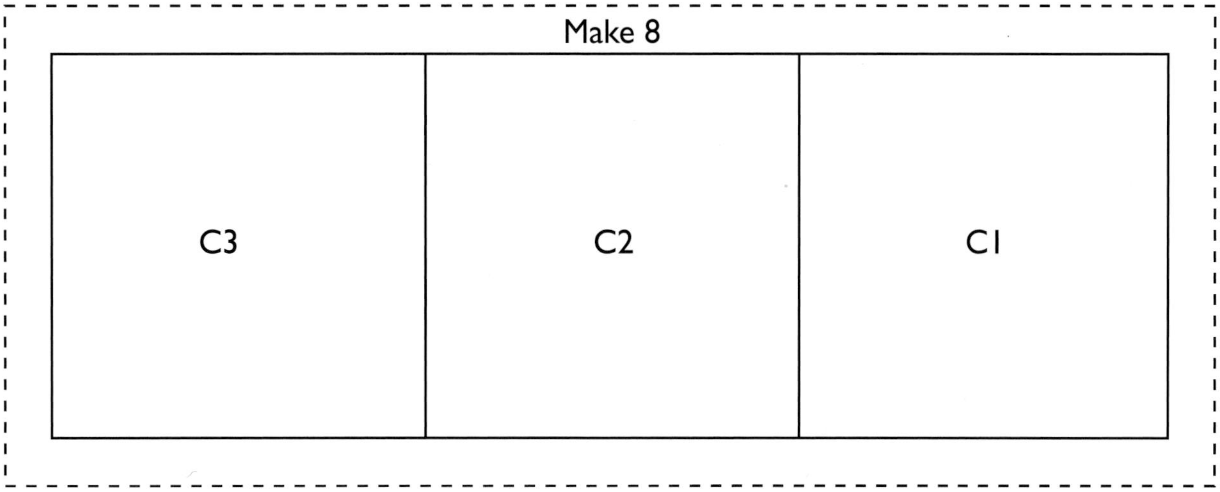

Make 8

C3	C2	C1

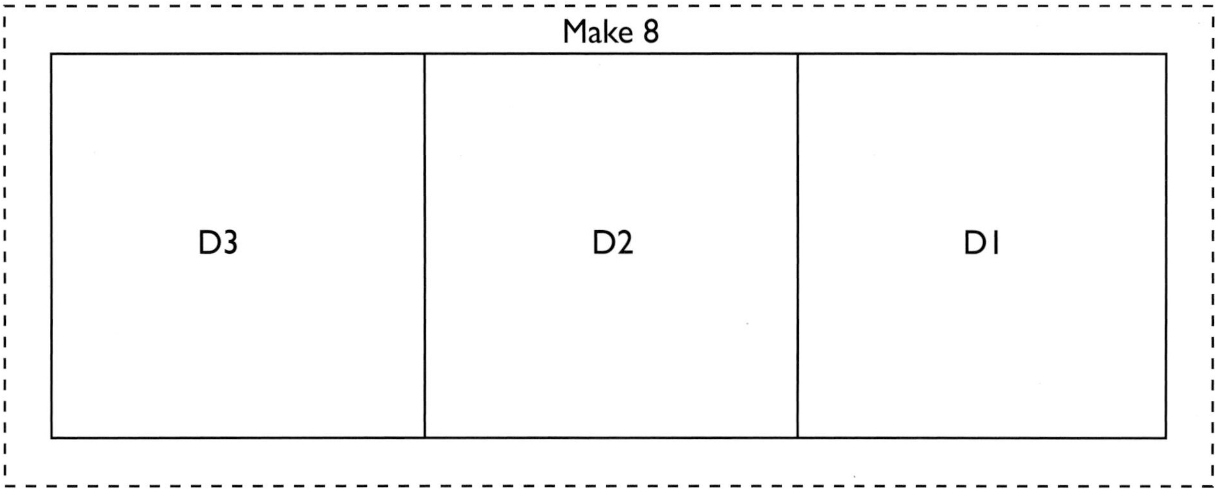

Make 8

D3	D2	D1

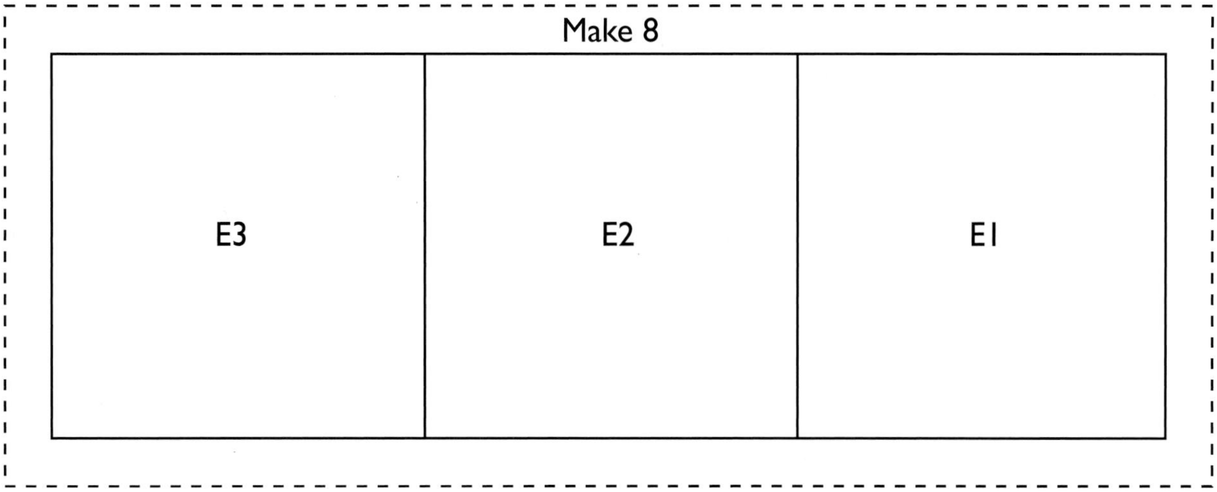

Make 8

E3	E2	E1

Wedding Ring Table Runner

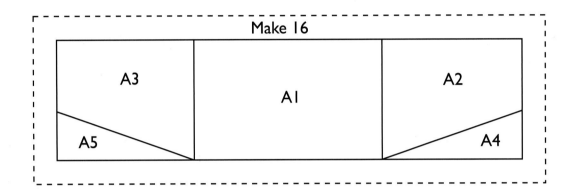

Make 16

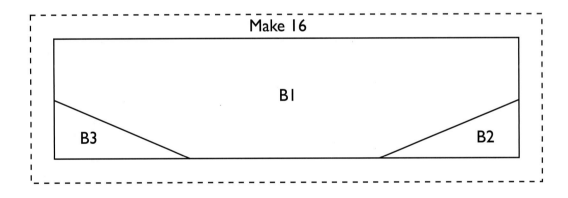

Make 16

Wedding Ring Table Runner

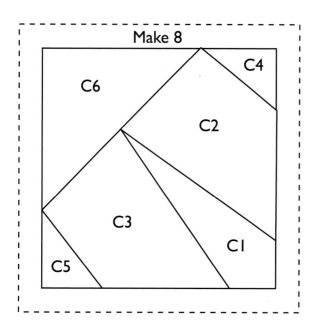

Make 8

C6 C4 C2 C3 C1 C5

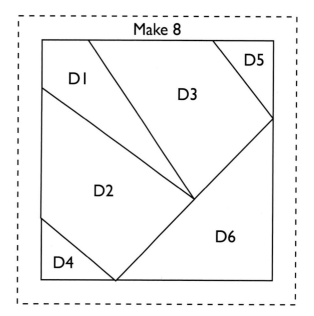

Make 8

D1 D5 D3 D2 D6 D4

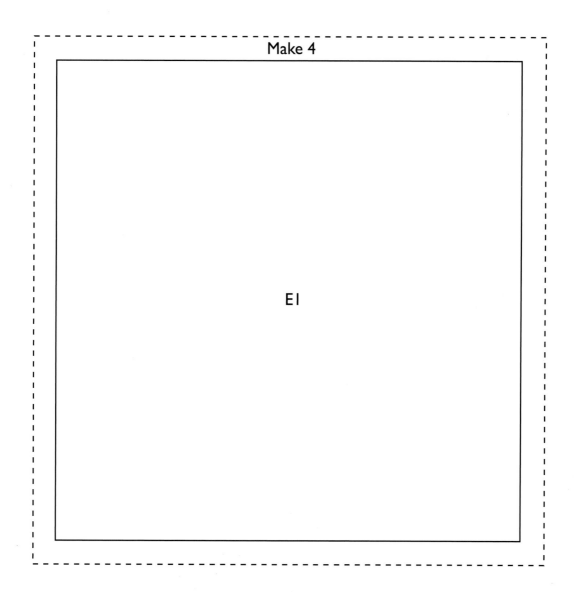

Make 4

E1

Wedding Ring Table Runner

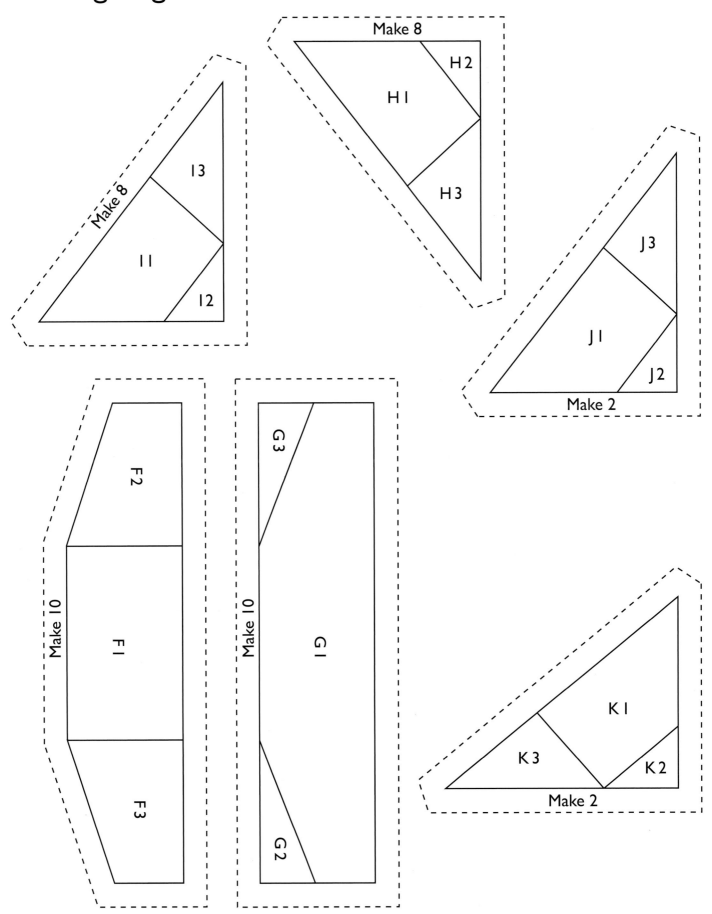

Make 8

H2

H1

H3

I3

I1

I2

Make 8

J3

J1

J2

Make 2

F2

F1

F3

Make 10

G3

G1

G2

Make 10

K1

K3

K2

Make 2

Miniature Wedding Ring

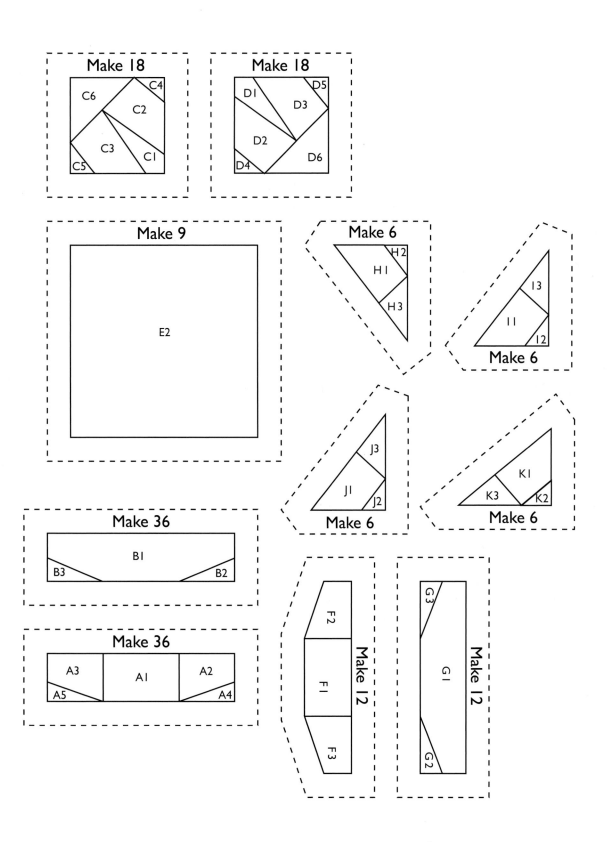

Solid Arc Wedding Ring Table Runner

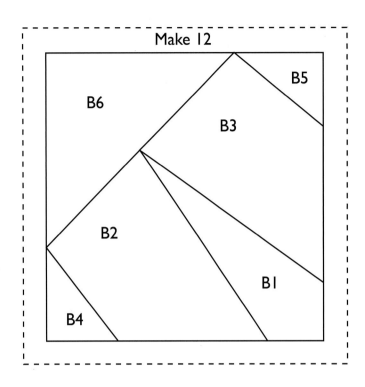

Make 12

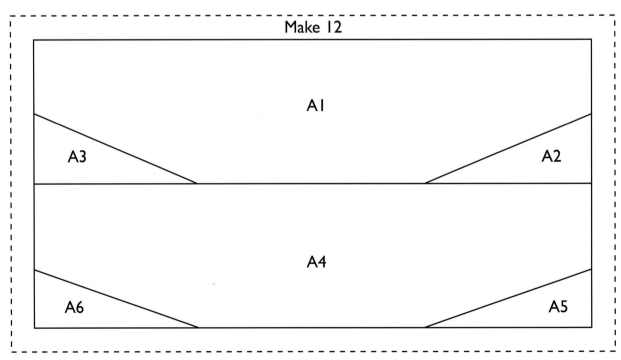

Make 12

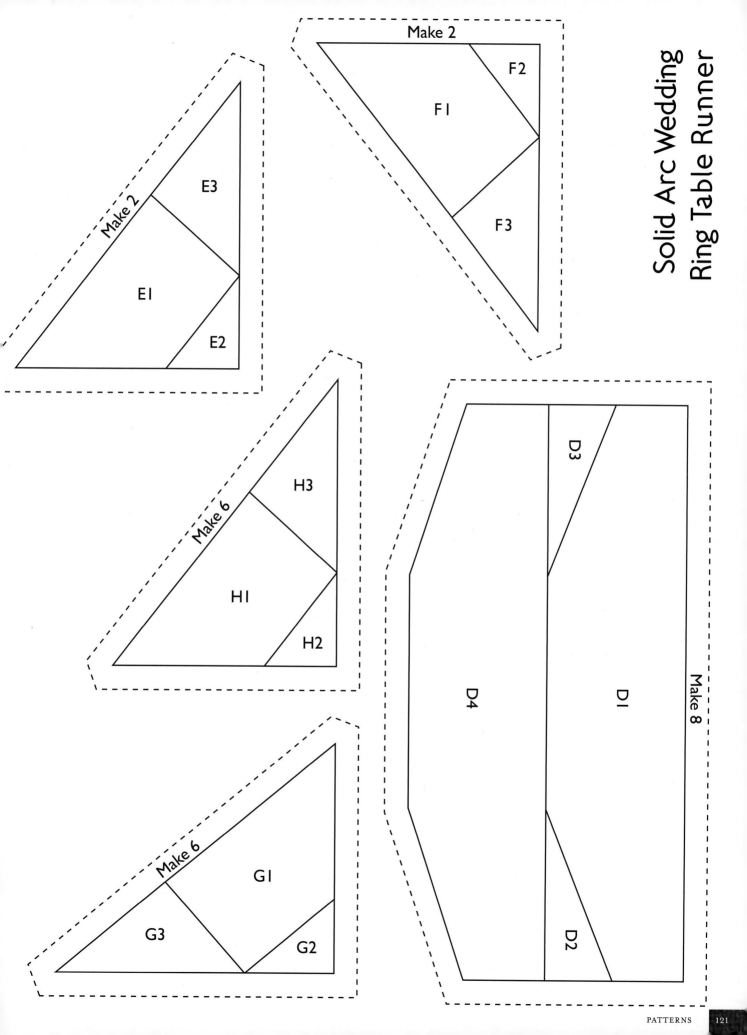

Solid Arc Wedding
Ring Table Runner

Make 2

F2

F1

F3

Make 2

E3

E1

E2

Make 6

H3

H1

H2

D3

D4

D1

Make 8

D2

Make 6

G1

G3

G2

Solid Arc Wedding Ring Table Runner

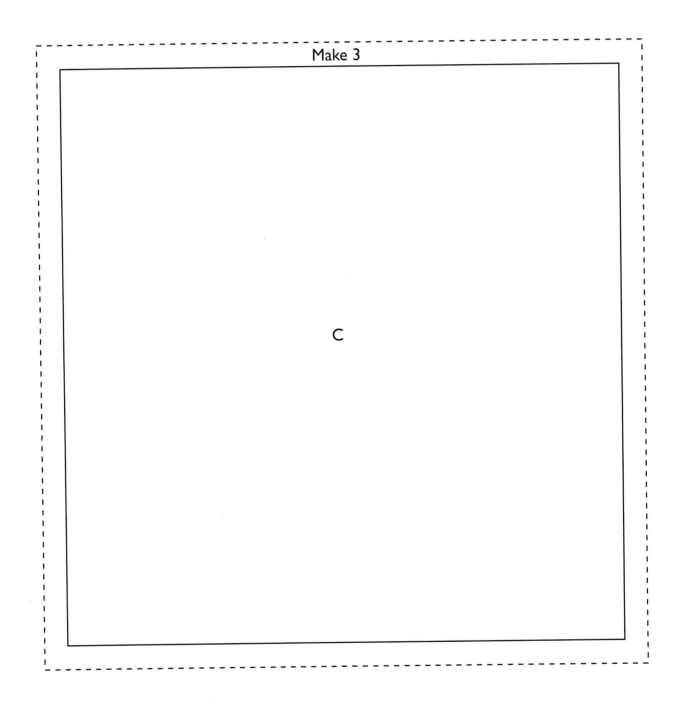

Make 3

C

Miniature Solid Arc Wedding Ring

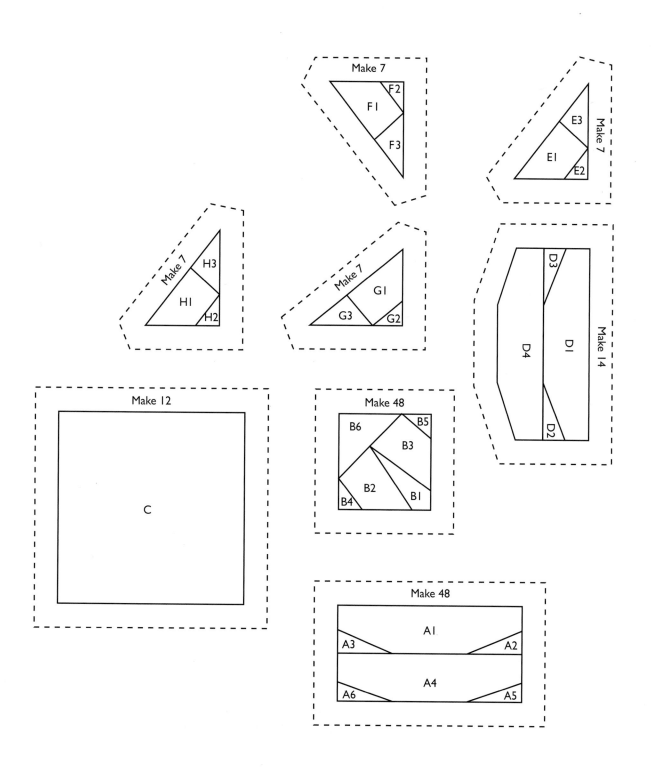

Resources

OTHER KANSAS CITY STAR BOOKS BY CAROLYN CULLINAN MCCORMICK

✳ *Carolyn's Paper Pieced Garden: Patterns for Miniature and Full-Sized Quilts*
— 2003

✳ *Hard Times, Splendid Quilts: A 1930s Celebration, Paper Piecing from The Kansas City Star*
— 2006

✳ *Quilts for Rosie: Paper Piecing Patterns from the '40s*
— 2008

MEASURING TOOLS:

Add-A-Quarter™
Add-Enough™
CM Designs, Inc
7968 Kelty Trail
Franktown, CO 80116
303-841-5920
Web: www.addaquarter.com

FABRICS:

In The Beginning Fabrics
8057 – 16th Ave NE
Seattle, WA 98115
Toll-Free: 888-523-1001
Web: www.inthebeginningfabrics.com

Reproductionfabrics.com
205 Haggerty Lane Suite 190
Bozeman, MT 59715
Phone: 406-586-1775
Toll-Free: 800-380-4611
Web: www.reproductionfabrics.com

Timeless Treasures
483 Broadway
New York, NY 10013
Phone: 212-226-1400
Web: www.ttfabrics.com

Batik Textiles
Toll-Free: 800-775-5030
Web: www.batiktextiles.com

Marcus Brothers Textiles, Inc.
980 Ave. of the Americas
New York, NY 10018
Phone: 212-354-8700
Web: www.marcusfabrics.com

BATTING:

The Warm Company
5529 – 186th Place SW
Lynnwood, WA 98037
Phone: 425-248-2424

THREAD:

Presencia®
P.O. Box 2409
Evergreen, CO 80437-2409
Toll Free: 866-277-6364
Web: www.presenciausa.com